5 Minutes with Jesus

A Fresh Infusion of JOY

Sheila Walsh

with Sherri Gragg

THOMAS NELSON
Since 1798

5 Minutes with Jesus: A Fresh Infusion of Joy

© 2016 Sheila Walsh

Published in Nashville, Tennessee, by Thomas Nelson. Thomas Nelson is a registered trademark of HarperCollins Christian Publishing, Inc.

Cover design by Katie Jennings Design

Thomas Nelson titles may be purchased in bulk for educational, business, fund-raising, or sales promotional use. For information, please e-mail SpecialMarkets@ ThomasNelson.com.

ISBN-13: 978-0-7180-3257-9

Printed in China

16 17 18 19 20 DSC 6 5 4 3 2 1

Introduction

How would you describe the amount of joy you feel today? Do you have a skip in your step, or are you dragging your feet? Maybe you're finding yourself smiling often . . . or maybe your heart is heavy, and joy seems hard to grasp.

We'd all like to be skipping and smiling—of course. But we've got *stuff*. Hard stuff. Whether it's a series of low-grade frustrations or some severe hardships, those things that can sadden, discourage, and flat-out exhaust us sometimes pile up and weigh us down.

Working as hard as you can for results that never come . . .

A broken relationship . . .

Shattered dreams . . .

An illness . . .

A bank account that's teetering toward the red . . .

Or maybe what burdens your heart more than anything else are reports of tragic suffering and violence. Perhaps you have looked long at the brokenness in our world, and you wonder how the light of God could possibly shine into such darkness.

Did you know Jesus warned us that this is *exactly* what we should expect from our sin-wounded world as the time draws near for His return? His caution to His disciples rings fresh and true even today, thousands of years later: "You will hear of wars . . . , but see to it that you are not alarmed. Such things must happen, but the end is still to come" (Matthew 24:6).

And on top of not being alarmed by hardships and strife, we are to "rejoice always" (1 Thessalonians 5:16).

The fact that Christians are able to live joyfully, no matter what, is a mystery, a *miracle* that can only come from the hand of God. The Bible has a lot to say about joy—what it looks like and where to find it. In the pages of Scripture, we see powerful examples of men and women of God who held tight to joy in desperate times. And we come to see that the call to joyful living brings God glory and is for our good. He wants to protect us from being consumed by discouragement and fear. And He wants to go beyond that.

Regardless of what comes your way today, Jesus wants your life to *overflow* with joy. Listen to His words: "I have told you these things so that you will be filled with my joy. Yes, your joy will overflow!" (John 15:11 NLT).

At this point you might be thinking, *Okay, that sounds great—but choosing joy isn't always that easy! Sometimes all I can see and think about are things that cause suffering and heartbreak. What's the secret? How do I begin to live joyfully, no matter what I'm going through?*

Taking some time out of each day to spend with Jesus, the Lover of your soul, is an important first step on your journey to joy. Make a point to be in His presence, in His Word, in His goodness and love. Remember that He brings life, restoration, and . . . joy.

You noticed in John 15 that Jesus talked about putting His joy in you, right? We can only imagine what there is yet to discover and experience when we open our hearts to Jesus and let Him fill us with the joy that can only come from Him!

And don't forget, the Spirit will help us. He'll be directing our thoughts and feelings to our great God and grounding us in Scripture's joy-giving truths. That long list of truths includes: God is with us and for us, our sins are forgiven, death has been defeated, heaven is on the horizon, God is working in and through us, and we get to receive and give His love.

So how about it? Will you join me in taking just five minutes out of your busy life to spend with God today? Let's walk this path together, sisters arm in arm, turning our eyes to the One we belong to, the One who loves us with an everlasting love.

Also, we've been building a supportive community at 5MinuteswithJesus.com, where you can find encouraging videos, images to share, and other reminders that just five minutes a day can transform our lives. We'd love to have you join us!

Come. Rest with Him for a moment. Listen to words of life.

And receive a fresh infusion of joy!

Choose Joy

What are your first thoughts in the morning?

    Coffee!

    A desperate wish for a little more sleep

    Anxiety about your job

    Worries for your family and friends

I can relate to all of these!

But I have learned a valuable secret: I have the power to stop those dark thoughts right in their tracks and choose joy instead. For me, the first step in this transformation is to turn my worry into gratitude.

I thank God for the bed I slept in and the roof over my head.

I thank Him that, in His faithfulness, He awakened me to a new day and has given me a fresh start.

I thank Him for my calling and the ways He uses it to grow me and provide for me.

I tell my heavenly Father how much I appreciate His promise to faithfully care for those I love.

We aren't able to control our circumstances or the difficulties each day brings, but as children of God we have great power to *choose* joy by focusing on the ways God blesses us.

Author Henri Nouwen warned us that "it is an ongoing temptation to think of ourselves as living under a curse. . . . Jesus came to bless us, not to curse us. But we must choose to receive that blessing and hand it on to others."[1]

And choosing joy in our lives is actually God's will for us, His children. He speaks very clearly through Paul in 1 Thessalonians 5:16–18: "Rejoice always, pray continually, give thanks in all circumstances; for this is God's will for you in Christ Jesus."

Ready to give it a try? Open your eyes to greet the new day and throw the doors of your heart open to joy by making a deliberate choice to embrace all the blessings God has lavished upon your life. Pour out your thanks to Him for each of His gifts, big and small, before you even put your feet on the floor.

> **There is power in your praise!**

ᴥ Five Minutes in the Word ᴥ

Let all who take refuge in you rejoice; let them ever sing for joy, and spread your protection over them, that those who love your name may exult in you. For you bless the righteous, O LORD; you cover him with favor as with a shield.

Psalm 5:11–12 ESV

Enter his gates with thanksgiving, and his courts with praise! Give thanks to him; bless his name! For the LORD is good; his steadfast love endures forever, and his faithfulness to all generations.

Psalm 100:4–5 ESV

LORD, be gracious to us; we long for you. Be our strength every morning, our salvation in time of distress.

Isaiah 33:2

Let the morning bring me word of your unfailing love, for I have put my trust in you. Show me the way I should go, for to you I entrust my life.

Psalm 143:8

Yet I will rejoice in the LORD, I will be joyful in God my Savior.

Habakkuk 3:18

Do You Know Who You Are?

Have you ever seen the movie *The Princess Diaries*? It's the story of an awkward teenage girl named Mia who can't seem to win at anything. Then one day her long-lost grandmother shows up with the earth-shattering announcement that young Mia is actually a princess!

Mia is quickly thrown into the process of being groomed to become the future queen. But Mia doesn't bring a lot to the table as a princess. She is short on grace, low on manners, knows nothing about governing a kingdom, and her hair is a complete disaster. Not much about her suggests she is worthy of the honorable title. But a princess she is, not because of her appearance or her ability to rule, but because of *who she is.* Mia is the only grandchild of the queen, and that is qualification enough.

We find a similar story in Scripture, but instead of a princess in the starring role, we have a long-lost prince named Mephibosheth. A descendant of King Saul, he was whisked away by his nurse to keep him safe when another family took over the kingdom. His very identity could mean death and danger.

Once David was on the throne, he sought out Mephibosheth, brought him into the palace, and treated him as one of his own sons. Why? Mephibosheth was the only living child of David's best friend, Jonathan. God gave this crippled man, who was a prince but felt so insignificant that he called himself a "dead dog" (2 Samuel 9:8), one incredibly happy ending.

Now for another example of royalty. Look in the mirror. Yes, look in the mirror. Do you know who *you* are? You might answer with your name or a role you think defines you—wife, daughter, mother, employee, volunteer. But the most significant answer is . . . you are a child of the King. And that's a capital *K* King!

The stories of Mia and Mephibosheth highlight a beautiful truth for children of the King. Our value in this life comes not from what we can accomplish or achieve but in *who we are*. When Jesus paid the price for our sins, God made us His very own daughters. We can joyfully cry out with the apostle John, "What marvelous love the Father has extended to us! Just look at it—we're called children of God! That's who we really are" (1 John 3:1 THE MESSAGE). God's love is a defining love—it changes everything.

I am a child of God.

⋯ Five Minutes in the Word ⋯

You are a chosen people, a royal priesthood, a holy nation, God's

special possession, that you may declare the praises of him who

called you out of darkness into his wonderful light. Once you

were not a people, but now you are the people of God; once you

had not received mercy, but now you have received mercy.

1 Peter 2:9–10

In Christ Jesus you are all children of God through faith.

Galatians 3:26

To all who did receive him, to those who believed in his name, he gave the

right to become children of God—children born not of natural descent,

nor of human decision or a husband's will, but born of God.

John 1:12–13

12

To me!

"I will be a Father to you, and you will be my sons and daughters, says the Lord Almighty."

2 Corinthians 6:18

Dear friends, now we are children of God, and what we will be has not yet been made known. But we know that when Christ appears, we shall be like him, for we shall see him as he is.

1 John 3:2

The Wonderful Ordinary

I was the least likely to be chosen.

Don't believe me? Here are some reasons why.

I walked in my sleep until I was almost eighteen. I couldn't go for more than two miles in a car without throwing up. The school nurse told my mom that I'd probably never be able to travel far from home. My father's suicide when he was thirty-four years old left a huge scar on my heart and a deep loneliness inside. The word that comes to mind when I think of the first thirty years of my life is *sad*. When someone you love with all your heart takes his or her life, it shatters your sense of worth. *Not worth staying around for . . . on the bargain pile . . .*

Even now, dear reader, as I write these words, I am again overwhelmed that God would use such a broken person to bring the hope and joy of Jesus to others. I grew up believing I had nothing to offer anyone.

Have you ever felt like you just didn't have anything

"special" enough to be used by God? Well, I have great news for you! You are *exactly* the kind of person God loves to call into His service.

You see, God doesn't look at things the way we do at all. We usually pick the gifted, the charming, the people who appear to have it all together for the big jobs. But God would rather use the ordinary people of this world to do His most important work.

I can't help but smile when I read Jesus' prayer about His disciples (and notice how Luke set it up): "Jesus, full of joy through the Holy Spirit, said, 'I praise you, Father, Lord of heaven and earth, because you have hidden these things [about the presence of God's kingdom and the fall of Satan] from the wise and learned, and revealed them to little children. Yes, Father, for this is what you were pleased to do'" (Luke 10:21).

I can just imagine the disciples hearing these words and thinking, *Well, thanks a lot. . . .* If they were beginning to have any delusions about how brilliant and fantastic they were, I guess that prayer cleared things right up!

Being likened to children rather than to "the wise and learned" might have been a hard truth for the disciples to hear, but it brings me a lot of comfort. I am so glad I don't have to be the smartest, most eloquent, most polished person in the room in order for God to use me in His kingdom work.

And if the miracle of God using people who don't have it all together—people like the disciples and me—can bring Jesus joy, how much joy should it bring to me?

> **God still calls the ordinary to do His kingdom work and know His joy!**

ꙮ Five Minutes in the Word ꙮ

God chose the foolish things of the world to shame the wise; God chose the weak things of the world to shame the strong. God chose the lowly things of this world and the despised things—and the things that are not—to nullify the things that are, so that no one may boast before him.

1 Corinthians 1:27–29

For Christ's sake, I delight in weaknesses, in insults, in hardships, in persecutions, in difficulties. For when I am weak, then I am strong.

2 Corinthians 12:10

[God] told me, "My grace is enough; it's all you need.
My strength comes into its own in your weakness."
2 Corinthians 12:9 THE MESSAGE

Don't let anyone look down on you because you are
young, but set an example for the believers in speech,
in conduct, in love, in faith and in purity.
1 Timothy 4:12

Our people must learn to devote themselves to
doing what is good, in order to provide for urgent
needs and not live unproductive lives.
Titus 3:14

Yet I Will Rejoice!

I was sitting on the Santa Monica Pier one sunny summer day when I saw the strangest thing. A seagull landed on the arm of the chair next to me, grabbed the lip gloss right out of the hand of the young woman who was about to use it, and flew off with it. She stood up and yelled at the feathered thief, "Are you kidding me? I just bought that!"

She plopped back down beside me and said, "Nothing in my life works!"

Have you ever felt like that? Have you ever found yourself saying, "There's no justice"?

The prophet Habakkuk would answer yes to those questions, but he would be commenting about more serious matters than lip gloss. He looked around his world and wondered what had happened to God's justice. So he turned to God, and he was brutally honest.

In Habakkuk 1, the prophet asked God hard questions about why He hadn't yet addressed the injustice and idolatry running rampant in Judah. When God responded, saying that He would indeed bring Judah to justice but He'd use their greatest enemies, the Babylonians, to do so, Habakkuk was dismayed! As far as Habakkuk was concerned, Judah's crimes paled in comparison to those of the Babylonians. He couldn't fathom why God would allow such a vile nation to prosper, much less use them to punish His chosen people. God assured Habakkuk that He would eventually bring His just judgment to the Babylonians as well, but Habakkuk would have to wait a very long time for that to happen.

By the final chapter, however, Habakkuk turned from questioning God to praising Him. He began his psalm by asking God to "in wrath remember mercy," and he ended it with some of the most beautiful words in Scripture: "Though the fig tree should not blossom, nor fruit be on the vines, the produce of the olive fail and the fields yield no food, the flock be cut off from the fold and there be no herd in the stalls, yet I will rejoice in the LORD; I will take joy in the God of my salvation" (Habakkuk 3:17–18 ESV).

Habakkuk knew dark days were ahead. And yet . . . he found that he had reason to rejoice.

Habakkuk had discovered a precious truth: when God is your treasure, you can lose everything and find that your reason to rejoice remains untarnished.

Don't wait until the difficult days come to begin finding joy in God alone. Start today. Then no matter what comes your way, you will find your joy unshaken.

ᕉ Five Minutes in the Word ᕇ

You make known to me the path of life; you will fill me with joy in
your presence, with eternal pleasures at your right hand.

Psalm 16:11

I delight greatly in the LORD; my soul rejoices in my God. For he
has clothed me with garments of salvation and arrayed me in a
robe of his righteousness, as a bridegroom adorns his head like
a priest, and as a bride adorns herself with her jewels.

Isaiah 61:10

One day spent in your house, this beautiful place of worship, beats
thousands spent on Greek island beaches. I'd rather scrub floors in the
house of my God than be honored as a guest in the palace of sin.

Psalm 84:10 THE MESSAGE

Through him you believe in God, who raised him from the dead
and glorified him, and so your faith and hope are in God.

1 Peter 1:21

This day is holy to our Lord. Do not grieve, for the joy of the LORD is your strength.

Nehemiah 8:10

Grace Welcomes You In

Mary Johnson lives next door to the young man who killed her teenage son. When she sees him at the mailbox, she doesn't glare and turn away. More often than not she says, "Boy, how come you haven't called to check on me?" Oshea laughs good-naturedly. You see, Mary, the mother of the boy he killed, is now like a mother to him.

It wasn't always so. A few years ago, while Oshea was in Stillwater Prison, Mary decided she wanted—after twelve long, angry years—to have a face-to-face meeting with the man who had taken her son's life. When she met Oshea and told him about her son, she began to cry. Oshea did the only thing he could think to do. He took the grieving mother into his arms to comfort her. Mary says she felt all of her anger just melt away.

Mary forgave Oshea, but that was just the beginning of the grace she offered him. She chose to love Oshea as her own son.

Oshea says he sometimes struggles to absorb Mary's forgiveness because he still hasn't totally forgiven himself—but, he says, he's learning from Mary.[2] Can you imagine the joy and hope Oshea must feel knowing the one he hurt the most has not only forgiven him but actually loves him?

Mary's kind of mercy—Jesus' kind of mercy—is overwhelming. Just ask Peter, one of Jesus' closest friends.

He'd vowed never to leave Jesus' side, but to save his own skin, Peter walked away from his Lord when Jesus most needed him. Peter must have wondered if Jesus could ever forgive him.

But then Jesus showed up on the beach one morning and called Peter to join Him for breakfast. And in that culture, inviting someone to a meal was never just about sharing the food. It was a sign of acceptance and . . . forgiveness.

Can you even imagine the immense relief and overwhelming joy Peter felt in that moment?

Peter had seen Jesus share meals with the most notorious sinners. Welcoming them into friendship like that was scandalous grace. And now Jesus spread the table of grace and acceptance and forgiveness for Peter: *Come. Have breakfast. I forgive you. I love you. Come, friend, and know My peace.*

Maybe you, like Peter, have wondered if your actions have taken you beyond the reach of grace. They haven't.

Hear Jesus' invitation: *Come! The table is spread for you. The Bread of Life has been broken for you. The blood of the new covenant has been shed for you.*

Jesus welcomes you with scandalous grace and calls you "friend." And the joy that comes with that kind of accepting, never-ending love can fill your heart to overflowing and will never end.

Grace sets the table for you and welcomes you in.

⁓ Five Minutes in the Word ⁓

You prepare a feast for me in the presence of my enemies. You honor me by anointing my head with oil. My cup overflows with blessings.

Psalm 23:5 NLT

[The Lord] said to me, "My grace is sufficient for you, for my power is made perfect in weakness." Therefore I will boast all the more gladly about my weaknesses, so that Christ's power may rest on me.

2 Corinthians 12:9

How priceless is your unfailing love, O God! People take refuge in the shadow of your wings. They feast on the abundance of your house; you give them drink from your river of delights. For with you is the fountain of life; in your light we see light.

Psalm 36:7–9

"Come now, let us reason together, says the LORD: though your sins are like scarlet, they shall be as white as snow; though they are red like crimson, they shall become like wool."

Isaiah 1:18 ESV

"His son said to him, 'Father, I have sinned against both heaven and you, and I am no longer worthy of being called your son.'
"But his father said to the servants, 'Quick! Bring the finest robe in the house and put it on him. Get a ring for his finger and sandals for his feet. And kill the calf we have been fattening. We must celebrate with a feast, for this son of mine was dead and has now returned to life. He was lost, but now he is found.'"

Luke 15:21–24 NLT

Not Always Easy

When my son, Christian, was a little boy, I asked him what he wanted to be when he grew up. He said, "Taller!"

When I was that age, I wanted to be a nurse in the slums of India—just as long as I could go home once a week for a bath!

What about you? When you were a child, what did you dream of becoming? I think we all share one thing: we want to know we have purpose. We want to know our lives will *count* for something!

Following God's plan is fulfilling and rewarding, but it's rarely easy. When we look at the lives of people in Scripture, we discover that God's call is often quite difficult. How do we find joy when the mission isn't an easy one?

Mary, the mother of Christ, knew more about God's demanding call than anyone, I suppose. When the angel Gabriel told her she would be the mother of the Messiah, she was most likely only thirteen or fourteen. Just a girl.

And she was a girl engaged to be married in a society that had zero tolerance for women who were pregnant out of wedlock. Mary could have been stoned. She most certainly would have been shunned by her community. It's likely her child would have been called horrible names. Her parents would have been devastated.

I can only imagine how terrified Mary must have been. It is hard to believe someone so young didn't complain or outright refuse. Today it's difficult to get the average fourteen-year-old to take out the trash without complaining!

But Mary didn't complain. Instead, she praised God for all He was doing through her life—despite how costly His plan would be to her. Listen to the words of her song:

> My spirit rejoices in God my Savior,
> for he has looked on the humble estate of his servant.
> For behold, from now on all generations will call me blessed;
> for he who is mighty has done great things for me,
> and holy is his name. (Luke 1:47–49 ESV)

Clearly Mary considered it an honor to be part of God's great work. What if, every day, you and I got out of bed and looked at our lives through this lens—that we are playing a beautiful, *honored* part in bringing God's glorious kingdom to this earth? Wouldn't that perspective fill us with energy and joy for the tasks at hand?

Mary's song also shows us that she had a long-term view of the situation. She knew that for a little while her reputation might be tarnished, but that ultimately "all generations" would call her blessed.

God's call on our lives may not be—in fact, probably won't be— easy, but when we keep a heavenly perspective on our circumstances, as Mary did, we too will be able to sing that our souls rejoice in God our Savior.

> *God has chosen you today to share*
> *His life with those around you!*

⋙ Five Minutes in the Word ⋘

Let us not grow weary in doing good, for in due season we will reap, if we do not give up. So then, as we have opportunity, let us do good to everyone, and especially to those who are of the household of faith.

Galatians 6:9–10 ESV

Fight the good fight of the faith. Take hold of the eternal life
to which you were called and about which you made the
good confession in the presence of many witnesses.

1 Timothy 6:12 ESV

After you have suffered a little while, the God of all grace, who has called
you to his eternal glory in Christ, will himself restore, confirm, strengthen,
and establish you. To him be the dominion forever and ever. Amen.

1 Peter 5:10–11 ESV

Do not be ashamed of the testimony about our Lord, nor of me his
prisoner, but share in suffering for the gospel by the power of God,
who saved us and called us to a holy calling, not because of our works
but because of his own purpose and grace, which he gave us in Christ
Jesus before the ages began, and which now has been manifested
through the appearing of our Savior Christ Jesus, who abolished
death and brought life and immortality to light through the gospel.

2 Timothy 1:8–10 ESV

She sets about her work vigorously; her arms are strong for her tasks.

Proverbs 31:17

The Great Gift

Nick Vujicic stood atop a table and faced a room full of mesmerized high school students. Some of them wept silently as they listened to this man who was born with no arms or legs proclaim joyfully, "I love life."[3]

If there is anyone who would seem to have a good reason to be joyless, it would be Nick. And yet he has chosen to embrace his life and the possibilities it offers as well as the gifts hidden in his suffering.

I think people like Nick are so compelling to us because we all want to know the secret of joy like his—joy that doesn't depend on physical perfection or life following some specific formula for success. We long for this because deep down we know that our journey throughout this life is fragile . . . inherently without guarantee. People like Nick show us that joy doesn't need to be tied to circumstances. They hold out the possibility of unshakeable joy that transcends suffering.

For many of us, joy is at a very low simmer. Even small

disappointments—a canceled lunch date with a friend, an unexpectedly high bill, finding the last piece of pie gone—can rob us of whatever joy we have. What makes people like Nick different?

I believe part of the secret to Nick's kind of resilient joy is to consider life, *all of life*, as a gift.

Every single day.

We can choose to be thankful for the gift of life no matter how difficult our path is because we are assured that God is with us in the middle of it and that He continues to bring blessings to our lives, even in our most painful moments.

I love this quote by Rowan Williams as he reflected on Jesus' final night before the cross: "When Jesus gives thanks at that moment before the breaking and spilling, before the wounds and the blood, it is as if he is connecting the darkest places of human experience with God the Giver; as if he is saying that even in these dark places God continues to give, and therefore we must continue to give thanks."[4]

Take some time today to reflect on a difficult season in which it wasn't easy for you to experience joy. What gifts was God still giving you? Perhaps it was the comfort of His presence or a powerful truth He revealed to you during that time. Grab a pen and a journal, and list any gifts that come to mind. Then spend some time thanking and praising God for His faithfulness, rejoicing that He never stops giving to us, even when our way is marked with sorrow.

> *Because God is good, we can worship Him always.*

⤳ Five Minutes in the Word ⤳

Every good gift and every perfect gift is from above, coming down from the Father of lights with whom there is no variation or shadow due to change. Of his own will he brought us forth by the word of truth, that we should be a kind of firstfruits of his creatures.

James 1:17–18 ESV

Bless the Lord, O my soul, and all that is within me, bless his holy name! Bless the Lord, O my soul, and forget not all his benefits, who forgives all your iniquity, who heals all your diseases, who redeems your life from the pit, who crowns you with steadfast love and mercy, who satisfies you with good so that your youth is renewed like the eagle's.

Psalm 103:1–5 ESV

There was nothing attractive about him, nothing to cause us
to take a second look. He was looked down on and passed
over, a man who suffered, who knew pain firsthand. One look
at him and people turned away. We looked down on him,
thought he was scum. But the fact is, it was our *pains he*
carried—our disfigurements, all the things wrong with us.

Isaiah 53:2–5 THE MESSAGE

Give thanks in all circumstances, for this is
God's will for you in Christ Jesus.

1 Thessalonians 5:18

Let the peace of Christ rule in your hearts, since as members
of one body you were called to peace. And be thankful.

Colossians 3:15

Don't Forget!

Have you ever walked into a room and forgotten why you went in there? Sometimes I back up to see if the reason will come back to me. It rarely does!

Or have you ever been introduced to someone and by the end of the "Nice to meet you" small talk (a whopping three or four minutes), you've forgotten her name? I can't count the times . . .

Well, like me, the Israelites had very short memories.

God had done mighty things for them. He had delivered them from slavery in Egypt and parted the Red Sea as they fled to safety. He had fed them with manna from heaven and empowered them to defeat their enemies. He had settled them in the promised land, the inheritance He had promised to their father Abraham.

And God knew that His mighty acts of deliverance would fade from His people's memories. So He went to great lengths to help them—and their children and their children's children—never to forget the amazing things He had done for His chosen people.

How? He gave them yearly feasts designed to remind them of important moments in their nation's history. God also commanded His people to teach their children about His mighty works. He urged them over and over again, *Never, ever forget all I have done for you.*

Sadly, some of them forgot anyway. Once they were settled in their new homes, their days were filled with raising crops and rearing children. The busyness of life crowded out people's remembrance of God and His work on their behalf.

But that wasn't true for everyone.

The person who wrote Psalm 136 remembered. Each line of the psalm recites a moment of God's goodness in Israel's history, paired with the joyous statement of praise, "His love endures forever."

We are much like Israel. It is all too easy for us to let hectic lives crowd out memories and thoughts about all God has done for us. Instead, our minds are cluttered with to-do lists and often weighed down by the ways—big and small—that life has gone "wrong."

I think today I'll write my own poem of praise to God

patterned after Psalm 136. I will first praise Him for who He is, and then I'll start listing all He has done for me.

And after each praise, I will remind myself of the sweetest truth of all, just as the psalmist did: "His love endures forever."

Will you join me?

> *Remember and rejoice in the*
> *faithfulness of God today.*

⤳Ⓖ Five Minutes in the Word ◯⤶

Give thanks to the LORD, for he is good. His love endures forever. Give
thanks to the God of gods. His love endures forever. Give thanks to
the Lord of lords: His love endures forever. . . . [Give thanks to him]
who spread out the earth upon the waters, His love endures forever.

Psalm 136:1–6

They celebrate your abundant goodness and joyfully
sing of your righteousness. The LORD is gracious and
compassionate, slow to anger and rich in love.

Psalm 145:7–8

When the LORD your God brings you into the land he swore to your fathers, to Abraham, Isaac and Jacob, to give you—a land with large, flourishing cites you did not build, houses filled with all kinds of good things you did not provide, wells you did not dig, and vineyards and olive groves you did not plant—then when you eat and are satisfied, be careful that you do not forget the LORD, who brought you out of Egypt, out of the land of slavery.

Deuteronomy 6:10–12

*On my bed I remember you; I think of you
through the watches of the night.*

Psalm 63:6

*I will remember the deeds of the LORD; yes, I will
remember your miracles of long ago.*

Psalm 77:11

The Light of the Spirit

Do you enjoy talking to God, Sheila?" she asked. I thought it was a very peculiar question.

"I do," I said. "Why do you ask?"

"When I watch you pray on television, you screw your forehead up as if you are about to have a root canal!" she said.

After I stopped laughing, I started thinking about her comment. I wondered if I had lost some of the joy I usually experienced when I was talking to God. I didn't know why that had become my default prayer face, but I knew I wanted a new one!

I began to look at all the ways the apostle Paul combined prayer and joy. The words *joy* and *rejoice* appear sixteen times in Paul's letter to the Philippians, and the first is this: "In all my prayers for all of you, I always pray with joy" (1:4).

Prayer is the place we meet with God. We bring our deepest sorrows and concerns before the Lord, and often we find that, under the brilliant light of His Spirit, we begin to see our circumstances differently. One reason that change of perspective happens is because as we pray, God meets our need—whatever it is—with His great provision: He fills our downcast souls with His joy.

That gift of joy is at the heart of prayer. It's not that we get up off our knees and find our world suddenly set in order. Instead, we rise to see it with new peace, new strength, new courage . . . and new joy.

Writer and Trappist monk Thomas Merton wrote this about prayer: "Prayer does not blind us to the world, but it transforms our vision of the world, and makes us see it, all men, and all the history of mankind in the light of God."[5]

Does your world feel dark today? Give God a chance to show you His brilliant light and speak to your heart. Let Him bring you the joy that comes from knowing that He who loves you unconditionally and forever is in absolute control of everything happening in your world.

> *Godly joy doesn't mean there is no sorrow. It means remembering that God is in control.*

⁓ Five Minutes in the Word ⁓

Be joyful in hope, patient in affliction, faithful in prayer.

Romans 12:12

The eyes of the Lord are on the righteous and his ears are attentive to
their prayer, but the face of the Lord is against those who do evil.

1 Peter 3:12

Devote yourselves to prayer, being watchful and thankful.

Colossians 4:2

Do not be anxious about anything, but in every situation, by
prayer and petition, with thanksgiving, present your requests to
God. And the peace of God, which transcends all understanding,
will guard your hearts and your minds in Christ Jesus.

Philippians 4:6–7

Dear friends, by building yourselves up in your most
holy faith and praying in the Holy Spirit.

Jude v. 20

Like Rain on Dry Ground

O h, how I wish I could have been one of those who drove through the Mojave Desert in the spring of 1998!

I've driven that long stretch of California road between Barstow and Needles several times, and that monotonous landscape makes the journey so boring. Vast, brown, empty . . . endless. It's the kind of place where time seems to stand still simply because each rock and every (occasional) dry bush look just like every other rock and bush.

But March 1998 was different. Seemingly overnight, everything changed. The ground that only the day before had been dry and lifeless was now completely covered with sunflowers. The glorious carpet stretched forty miles long and ten miles wide. Travelers pulled their cars over to the side of the road in awe. Entranced, they exited their cars and wandered about in the ocean of yellow blossoms.

It was a rare event brought about by an unusual, deep, soaking rain that had fallen the previous autumn. For years the sunflower seeds had been lying dormant on the desert floor. Then came the rain—it was the real hero. Suddenly the seeds were freed to come to life and bloom a glorious gold. What a beautiful picture of how the Holy Spirit produces joy in our lives!

There are times when I get everything backward. I set harsh standards for myself. I push myself to work harder, get more done, *be more*! And while it's good to grow and reach for goals, my preoccupation with performance can leave me feeling exhausted and empty . . . not unlike a brown, lifeless desert.

But my God of grace doesn't offer performance-based joy. He understands that I, like the sunflower seeds, am scattered hopelessly about in a parched and weary land, that I am dry and dead apart from Him. And He doesn't let me stay that way.

God's Spirit is the life-giving, *joy*-producing rain that I so desperately need.

So today, instead of focusing so much on producing more and being more, I think I will take a deep breath, open my heart to God, and ask Him for a fresh outpouring of His Holy Spirit and the joy He brings. I am confident God will be faithful.

Won't you join me? Let's stand with our arms outstretched and faces lifted toward heaven, and ask the Holy Spirit to rain down on us anew.

> *Holy Spirit, rain on me today and fill me with joy!*

⋘ Five Minutes in the Word ⋙

The fruit of the Spirit is love, joy, peace, forbearance, kindness, goodness, faithfulness, gentleness and self-control. Against such things there is no law.

Galatians 5:22–23

He saved us, not because of righteous things we had done, but because of his mercy. He saved us through the washing of rebirth and renewal by the Holy Spirit, whom he poured out on us generously through Jesus Christ our Savior, so that, having been justified by his grace, we might become heirs having the hope of eternal life.

Titus 3:5–7

"Others, like seed sown on good soil, hear the word, accept it, and produce a crop—some thirty, some sixty, some a hundred times what was sown."

Mark 4:20

He brought out his people with rejoicing, his chosen ones with shouts of joy.

Psalm 105:43

May he be like rain falling on a mown field, like showers watering the earth.

Psalm 72:6

Finding Joy in
Our Yes to God

Jonah was not a happy prophet.

God had given Jonah the assignment of his worst nightmares when He told him to go to Nineveh and preach a message of repentance. Encouraging the Ninevites to turn to God was the *last* thing any good Israelite would want to do. These Assyrians were brutal, relentless invaders. Jonah would have much preferred that God wipe them off the map instead of saving them. So, instead of going to Nineveh, Jonah hopped aboard a ship sailing in the *opposite* direction.

But Jonah couldn't run from God. The almighty Lord sent a violent storm and then, when the sailors tossed the fleeing prophet off the boat, He sent a great fish to swallow him. After it spit him out, Jonah had another chance to obey.

And obey Jonah did. He preached repentance to the

Ninevites and—much to his annoyance—repent is exactly what they did!

Soon after, we find Jonah sitting on a hillside under a wilted plant in the burning sun, not talking to God. Even though God had motivated Jonah to obey by putting him in a three-day time-out in a fish's belly, Jonah still chose not to be happy about it.

Obedience is hard sometimes, isn't it? We each have that rebellious streak, passed down to us through our first parents, Adam and Eve: we just want to do our own thing.

But Scripture gives us solid reasons to believe that obeying God will bring great joy!

Listen to Psalm 19:7–8: "The law of the LORD is perfect, reviving the soul; the testimony of the LORD is sure, making wise the simple; the precepts of the LORD are right, rejoicing the heart; the commandment of the LORD is pure, enlightening the eyes" (ESV).

The psalmist was saying that God's rules bring joy to our hearts. That might seem a little strange at first, and part of the reason may be rooted further back than you know. You see, the Greeks—who gave us the original translation of the New Testament—have only one word for *law*, and it has a negative connotation. The Hebrew people had a very different perspective: their word for God's Law, the precious Torah, was much more positive. Jews, then and today, consider the Torah a great gift from God, given to people to teach them how to "hit the mark" in life.[6]

Do you believe that God loves you and that His purposes are for your good? Then offer Him your obedience. Not a *grudging* obedience like Jonah's, but a heartfelt and unreserved yes to His commands. In acting on your yes—in obeying God's commands— you will know joy in your heart.

> *Discover the undiluted joy in*
> *living to please the Father!*

✺ Five Minutes in the Word ✺

All of the paths of the LORD are steadfast love and faithfulness,
for those who keep his covenant and his testimonies.

Psalm 25:10 ESV

I rejoice in following your statues as one rejoices in great riches. I meditate
on your precepts and consider your ways. I delight in your decrees.

Psalm 119:14–16

Great peace have those who love your law, and nothing can make them stumble. I wait for your salvation, Lord, and I follow your commands. I obey your statutes, for I love them greatly. I obey your precepts and your statutes, for all my ways are known to you.

Psalm 119:165–168

Open my eyes that I may see wonderful things in your law.

Psalm 119:18

As the eyes of slaves look to the hand of their master, as the eyes of a female slave look to the hand of her mistress, so our eyes look to the Lord our God, till he shows us his mercy.

Psalm 123:2

Complete Healing

As a mom I just knew that something was wrong. I couldn't quite put my finger on what it might be, but I knew that Christian was sick. I took him to his pediatrician, who, after briefly examining him, told me he thought Christian was fine and sent us home. Moms are not so easily appeased, though . . .

I made another appointment and asked the doctor to do a more thorough exam. This time the doctor agreed that something was wrong, and he ran some bloodwork. He told me that he'd have the results the following morning. I asked him what it looked like to him. He said, "It could be a number of things." He was a family friend, so I pushed him for more information. That's when I heard the bone-chilling word *leukemia*.

My heart sank in my chest as I considered what might lie ahead for my son. Like thousands of mothers before me, I asked God to give the disease—or whatever it was—to *me* instead of my boy.

That was one of the longest nights of my life.

But in the morning, we received the relieving report that Christian was just anemic, a very treatable condition.

A few weeks later I shared this story from a stage. Afterward, a mom came up to me and said, "I got the other phone call." I felt so ashamed that my good news had been salt in someone else's wound. Realizing what I was thinking, this dear woman said, "No! Don't feel bad. I just want you to know that whether you get the answer you pray for or the answer you dread, God is faithful."

I looked in her eyes and saw the kind of steadfast strength and deep joy that only Christ can give.

Illness, whether physical, mental, emotional, or spiritual, has such power to weigh heavily on our hearts because deep inside we know that it was *just never meant to be this way*. God made this world in beautiful perfection, but when our first parents, Adam and Eve, sinned, sickness and death disfigured God's flawless creation.

Jesus' ministry on earth was a hands-on demonstration of what it looks like when God begins to break the curse; His death, burial, and glorious resurrection provided the ultimate cure for our "sin disease."

And that disease will be ultimately defeated when Jesus returns. On that promised day, our healing—physical, mental, emotional, and spiritual—will be complete and eternal.

Who knows? Maybe it will even be today!

⚘Five Minutes in the Word⚘

Praise the LORD, my soul, and forget not all his benefits—who forgives all your sins and heals all your diseases, who redeems your life from the pit and crowns you with love and compassion.

Psalm 103:2–4

[Jesus] was pierced for our transgressions, he was crushed for our iniquities; the punishment that brought us peace was on him, and by his wounds we are healed.

Isaiah 53:5

LORD my God, I called to you for help, and you healed me.

Psalm 30:2

He heals the brokenhearted and binds up their wounds.

Psalm 147:3

The prayer offered in faith will make the sick person well; the Lord will raise them up. If they have sinned, they will be forgiven.

James 5:15

Joy from Justice

Fifty beds lined the driveway of Heartline Ministries in Port-au-Prince, Haiti. This makeshift field hospital ministered to the suffering in the days and weeks following the devastating earthquake of 2010. Among the badly wounded was a small boy named Emmanuel . . . *God with us.*

Emmanuel's mother was by his side. The same earthquake that had left her little boy's body broken and scarred had taken the lives of her other three children. She was utterly shattered by the grief.

Yet every night she raised her voice to lead the entire hospital in worship to God. Grown men were reduced to tears at the sight and the sound.

Time passed. Emmanuel's body healed, and he and his mom moved south to try to start over. One day the missionaries at Heartline received a call from her: she was expecting another child. Arrangements were made for her and Emmanuel to come to Heartline's maternity center.

There she delivered a son, a miracle of redemption. She named him Raphael . . . *Healing God.*

The missionary midwives of Heartline Ministries love to tell the story of Emmanuel and his mother. They point to it as a powerful example of their personal experience of Proverbs 21:15—"When justice is done, it brings joy to the righteous but terror to evildoers."

Perhaps using the word *justice* here seems odd to you, but I assure you, justice matters deeply to God. He cares passionately that some of His children suffer crushing poverty. It breaks His heart that more women die in childbirth in Haiti than anywhere else in the Western Hemisphere.

Whenever we, like the missionaries at Heartline, humbly work to meet the needs of people like Emmanuel and his mother, we are partnering with God in furthering His justice.

It is a partnership that demands sacrifice—the sacrifice of our self-interest, pride, and conveniences—but Proverbs promises when we see that "justice is done," we will experience joy.

Ask God to open your eyes and heart today to those who are suffering from injustice. Seek His guidance as to where and how you can partner with Him to be a part of the solution. I promise you, He is already at work! The Lord's justice and joy are always on the move. All you have to do is get on board.

> **Shine the light of Christ by serving those in the darkest places.**

⋙ Five Minutes in the Word ⋘

Do not pervert justice or show partiality. Do not accept a bribe, for a bribe blinds
the eyes of the wise and twists the words of the innocent. Follow justice and justice
alone, so that you may live and possess the land the LORD your God is giving you.

Deuteronomy 16:19–20

Do not deprive the foreigner or the fatherless of justice,
or take the cloak of the widow as a pledge.

Deuteronomy 24:17

The LORD is righteous, he loves justice; the upright will see his face.

Psalm 11:7

"Learn to do right; seek justice. Defend the oppressed. Take up
the cause of the fatherless; plead the case of the widow."

Isaiah 1:17

"When you reap the harvest of your land, do not reap to the very edges
of your field or gather the gleanings of your harvest. Do not go over your
vineyard a second time or pick up the grapes that have fallen. Leave
them for the poor and the foreigner. I am the LORD your God."

Leviticus 19:9–10

A Life of Love

Over dinner one night my friend told me of her son's confusion about Christ's whereabouts.

"We had explained to Myles that after he'd invited Jesus into his heart, He would stay there," she said. "I read him the verse that says if we abide in Him, He will abide in us. Myles seemed to get it at first, but later that night I realized we had a little work to do!"

She told me that after they had said their prayers and she'd kissed him good night, she heard a noise coming from her son's room. Tiptoeing down the hall, she listened at the door.

"Jesus! Jesus! I'm abiding!" Myles was shouting, looking down at the front of his pajama top.

"Are you okay?" she said, popping her head inside his room.

"I've been calling to Jesus, Mom, but He won't say a thing!" Myles replied.

Abiding in Christ can be confusing—both to children and to adults.

To help us understand the kind of intimate relationship God the Father wants to have with His children, Jesus used images from agriculture. He proclaimed that He is the "vine" and His followers are the "branches" (John 15:5). The only way to bear fruit, Jesus explained, is to stay connected to His love, and the only way to stay connected to His love is to obey His commands.

"Which commands?" you might ask. In John 15:12, Jesus gave us the answer: He wants us to love one another as He loves us.

Sometimes it seems that all of Scripture keeps coming back to those two things, doesn't it? Love God and love one another. Obedience to these commands is both the simplest and most difficult work of our lives, but this call to love is the gospel. I think we have all had moments when we wish God had given us a nice checklist of things to do instead:

Give money to the church. *Check*.
Pray before meals. *Check*.
Go to church. *Check*.

But the kingdom of God has never been about external performance. It's all about the heart!

Jesus has an underlying motive when He commands us to love (and of course, He has our best interest in mind): "I have told you this so that my joy may be in you and that your joy may be complete" (John 15:11).

Complete joy? Amazing!

Take a moment today just to ask God to fill your heart with greater love for Him, and for the people around you as well. Then determine to stay connected to Jesus and live a life of love. And you'll find a life of joy.

> *A life of loving God and others is a life of joy.*

⟩ᜥ Five Minutes in the Word ᜥ⟨

"As the Father has loved me, so have I loved you. Now remain in my love. If you keep my commands, you will remain in my love, just as I have kept my Father's commands and remain in his love. I have told you this so that my joy may be in you and that your joy may be complete."

John 15:9–11

Keep yourselves in God's love as you wait for the mercy of
our Lord Jesus Christ to bring you to eternal life.

Jude v. 21

I am not writing you a new command but one we have had from
the beginning. I ask that we love one another. And this is love:
that we walk in obedience to his commands. As you have heard
from the beginning, his command is that you walk in love.

2 John vv. 5–6

This is love for God: to keep his commands. And his commands are
not burdensome, for everyone born of God overcomes the world.

1 John 5:3–4

Mercy, peace and love be yours in abundance.

Jude v. 2

A Divine Mission

After the death of my mother-in-law, Eleanor, Barry and I invited his father, William, to move in with us. It was clear to both of us that he was not the kind of man who would have done well living alone. Christian was so excited to have his papa living under the same roof, and the feeling was gloriously mutual.

William was an absolute joy to have around. He helped me cook meals, and he loved to entertain us with his repertoire of stories about growing up in Charleston, South Carolina.

He had a very easygoing nature, but one night at supper he snapped at me. It was so unlike him, but I knew that his knees had been bothering him, so I put it down to that.

He excused himself and disappeared into his bedroom. When he hadn't come out after an hour, I went to check on him. I knocked on the door, and he invited me to come in. He was sitting on the edge of his bed with his suitcase packed, so I asked him where he was going.

"Home," he said. "You probably want me to leave now."

"Dad, this is your home now," I reminded him. "We used to be a family of three—Barry, Christian, and I—but now we're a family of four. We all get to make mistakes."

I hugged him tight as tears ran down his face. And I realized in that moment that William had experienced very little grace in his life.

Christlike love and grace are the most powerful forces in the world. They break through hard hearts that no amount of lecturing could even begin to crack. Grace and love melt sin-forged habits. They empower the fallen to get up again. And they compel hearts to turn toward redemption and try . . . just one more time.

We, the children of the great King, are the bearers of this divine inheritance of grace and love. That's why God has given each of us this mission: *Be My ambassador. Pass on My grace and love!*

What a privilege to be called and empowered by God to carry out such an important mission! The Almighty has entrusted us to shine the light of His truth into lives that are darkened by habits they can't seem to break, regrets they can't seem to leave in the past, and pain that keeps haunting them.

Look around you today. Who in your circle of influence needs the message of God's grace? Be Christ's ambassador today and reap a harvest of joy!

> *What a privilege—and what a joy—*
> *to share God's grace and love!*

✦ Five Minutes in the Word ✦

We proclaim to you what we have seen and heard, so that you also may have fellowship with us. And our fellowship is with the Father and with his Son, Jesus Christ. We write this to make our joy complete.

1 John 1:3–4

We are therefore Christ's ambassadors, as though God were making his appeal through us. We implore you on Christ's behalf: Be reconciled to God.

2 Corinthians 5:20

It was revealed to them that they were not serving themselves but you, when they spoke of the things that have now been told you by those who have preached the gospel to you by the Holy Spirit sent from heaven. Even angels long to look into these things.

1 Peter 1:12

We know, brothers and sisters loved by God, that he has chosen you, because our gospel came to you not simply with words but also with power, with the Holy Spirit and deep conviction. You know how we lived among you for your sake.

1 Thessalonians 1:4–5

How can anyone preach unless they are sent? As it is written: "How beautiful are the feet of those who bring good news!"

Romans 10:15

Parties in Heaven

I f you had bumped into Brian Welch, former lead guitar-
ist for the band Korn, before his encounter with Christ,
you might have given him a wide berth. After all, he was
covered in tattoos and addicted to drugs. His fans, however,
thought he had everything. They didn't know that behind
the money, women, and fame there was a man at the end of
his rope.

One night, immediately after doing the drugs he so
hated, Welch turned his face toward heaven and prayed,
"Jesus, if You are real, You have got to take these drugs from
me. Come into my life. Come into my heart. You know I want
to quit. You know I want to be a good dad for my kid. She lost
her mother to drugs, and she's going to lose me if I don't quit.
Amen."

Brian sat silently, waiting for God's reply.

Suddenly, the love and acceptance of Brian's heavenly
Father flooded his heart. "I felt so much fatherly love from

heaven. . . . It was so powerful that the next day I threw away all my drugs."[7]

In Luke 15, Jesus told three parables to illustrate the joy that takes place in heaven every time someone like Brian surrenders to the Father's saving love. Jesus talked about a lost sheep, a lost coin, and, finally, a lost son. Three very different stories with two things in common: First, each of these lost ones is utterly helpless to save themselves. Second, when each is found, there is great rejoicing all around.

Have you ever stopped to consider how much God loves you? Or that when you surrendered your life to Him, He was so filled with joy that He threw a party in your honor in heaven? God invites us to be part of that kind of celebration by sharing with others the life we have in Christ.

You don't have to be a Bible teacher or a world-class evangelist to share the love story of your life, the one with Jesus, your Savior. All you have to do is share the truth that set you free. So invite friends who don't know Jesus over for dinner or take them to church. Look for opportunities simply to tell the story of how the Father's love rescued you, just as it rescued Brian. That's what people are hungry to hear. No one needs religion, but we all long for relationship. That's why Jesus came.

Let's keep giving heaven reasons to party!

◈ Five Minutes in the Word ◈

*"There will be more rejoicing in heaven over one sinner who repents
than over ninety-nine righteous persons who do not need to repent."*

Luke 15:7

"The Son of Man came to seek and to save the lost."

Luke 19:10

*"Learn what this means: 'I desire mercy, not sacrifice.' For
I have not come to call the righteous, but sinners."*

Matthew 9:13

*Since we are receiving a kingdom that cannot be shaken, let us be
thankful, and so worship God acceptably with reverence and awe.*

Hebrews 12:28

*The Lord will rescue me from every evil attack and will bring me safely
to his heavenly kingdom. To him be glory for ever and ever. Amen.*

2 Timothy 4:18

Be a Cheerleader

Maybe I'm getting too personal, but I'm going to ask anyway: How do you store your Christmas decorations eleven months of the year?

We shove ours into a closet . . . and I do mean shove! Oh, we always intend to sort and neatly organize the ribbons, glass ornaments, lights, and bows. But because that—for whatever reason—never happens, every November I face the unruly tangle that is the Walsh Christmas. Except for one box!

In that box is every ornament our son has made since he was a child. Some he made at school; a few were family projects. All of them prompt sweet memories of special moments with Christian that I treasure.

In fact, moments like those are among the countless opportunities for pure, undiluted joy that motherhood has brought into my life. Witnessing my son's achievements as well as helping him get there, especially when he wanted to give up, are some of my brightest memories.

Now that Christian is an adult, I have the joy of seeing him pour into his friends' lives. He has always had a tender heart, and I love watching the ways he encourages others.

God has tucked great joy into the act of helping our brothers and sisters and supporting them on their journey. It is easy to think of our walk with Christ in purely personal terms—about what He is doing in *us* and in *our* lives—but the Christian walk is not a solitary pilgrimage. Each of us is part of the body of Christ, so every step we take is alongside our brothers and sisters in the Lord.

And we have a responsibility to one another as we travel through life: to encourage each other in our faith. We are to be iron sharpening iron. We are to "spur one another on toward love and good deeds" (Hebrews 10:24).

With these responsibilities comes the possibility of great joy, just as with parenting. Investing ourselves in each other's growth in Christ will lead to joyful celebrations of deepening faith.

Do you realize how valuable you are to your family in Christ? We *need* each other. Let's choose today to be each other's greatest cheerleaders and most faithful supporters. Then what joy we will have as we witness each other fall more deeply in love with Him day by day!

⋰⋱ Five Minutes in the Word ⋰⋱

What is our hope, our joy, or the crown in which we will
glory in the presence of our Lord Jesus when he comes?
Is it not you? Indeed, you are our glory and joy.

1 Thessalonians 2:19–20

How can we thank God enough for you in return for all the
joy we have in the presence of our God because of you?

1 Thessalonians 3:9

Just as each of us has one body with many members, and these
members do not all have the same function, so in Christ we, though
many, form one body, and each member belongs to all the others.

Romans 12:4–5

Be devoted to one another in love. Honor one another above yourselves.

Romans 12:10

Grow in the grace and knowledge of our Lord and Savior Jesus
Christ. To him be glory both now and forever! Amen.

2 Peter 3:18

Keeping On for the Prize of Joy

It turns out the *fifth* time's the charm.

Well, at least for Diana Nyad that was the case. On September 2, 2013, sixty-four-year-old Diana completed her record-setting swim from Havana, Cuba, to Key West, Florida. I watched the news coverage in amazement as people wrapped blankets around the battered but victorious swimmer. With four other failed attempts in her wake, she pressed on for fifty-three hours, braving sharks, jellyfish, and relentless winds.

"With all the experience I have, especially in this ocean, I never knew I would suffer the way I did," she said after finishing.

Hers is a feat most of us find incomprehensible. Whenever I hear about someone like Diana, enduring the unimaginable to accomplish the impossible, I want to know what kept her pressing on long past the moment she wanted to quit.

Diana was motivated by a dream. She was eight years old when she first stood on the shore of Cuba and gazed out across the ocean. The shores of Florida rested far beyond her ability to see them, but she dreamed of swimming the distance one day.

She never let this dream go. More than five decades later, she reached for it with each and every stroke. The dream kept her swimming past the exhaustion and pain.[8]

For the joy of realizing her lifelong dream, Diana was willing to endure the suffering.

Have you ever wondered what motivated Jesus to endure the suffering and shame of the cross? Scripture tells us that when Christ faced the cross He had a specific goal in mind.

Jesus endured the cross for the sake of joy. The meaning of *endured* in the original language is "to stay in a place beyond the expected length of time." That's what Diana did. That's what Christ did for you and me.

Listen to Hebrews 12:1–2: "Let us run with perseverance the race marked out for us, fixing our eyes on Jesus, the pioneer and perfecter of faith. For the joy set before him he endured the cross, scorning its shame, and sat down at the right hand of the throne of God."

As Jesus faced the cross, knowing all the suffering and shame it would bring, He kept His eyes firmly on the prize of joy that would be His when His blood paid all our debts. His perfect life, death, and resurrection broke sin's curse and forever swallowed up death.

Jesus endured it all for the joy of making you, making me, His *own*.

Hallelujah! What a Savior!

> **The greater the endurance, the deeper the joy.**

✜ Five Minutes in the Word ✜

On this mountain he will destroy the shroud that enfolds all peoples, the sheet that covers all nations; he will swallow up death forever. The Sovereign LORD will wipe away the tears from all faces; he will remove his people's disgrace from all the earth. The LORD has spoken.

Isaiah 25:7–8

The message of the cross is foolishness to those who are perishing,
but to us who are being saved it is the power of God.
1 Corinthians 1:18

May I never boast except in the cross of our Lord Jesus Christ, through
which the world has been crucified to me, and I to the world.
Galatians 6:14

God was pleased to have all his fullness dwell in him, and through
him to reconcile to himself all things, whether things on earth or things
in heaven, by making peace through his blood, shed on the cross.
Colossians 1:19–20

"I am the Living One; I was dead, and now look, I am alive for
ever and ever! And I hold the keys of death and Hades."
Revelation 1:18

Always Enough

I remember exactly where I was standing when I heard the news that Diana, Princess of Wales, had been killed in a car crash in Paris. It was hard to take in: such life and beauty had been snuffed out in a moment. The image that is seared into my memory, though, is from a few days later as her two brave boys walked behind her casket. The pageantry and the grandeur of the official funeral was made starkly human by the sight of an envelope resting in the white roses on her casket. On the envelope was the word *Mummy* in a child's handwriting; in it, a note from twelve-year-old Harry.

King David would most certainly have understood the pain of such loss. He wrote so many of his psalms in moments of heartbreak, but because he was the king, he was rarely granted the kindness of walking through his grief behind closed doors.

Agonizing moments played out in the public eye:

> Those long years when Saul hunted him.
>
> His best friend Jonathan's death.
>
> His great sin with Bathsheba and then the death of their young son.
>
> His brutal betrayal by his son Absalom.
>
> And then his grief over Absalom's death.

But over and over, David's psalms show how he clung desperately to God and then came out the other side of grief to experience joy again.

Whether our most painful moments are private or public, we, like David, will find refuge and comfort in God alone. There, in the arms of our Father, we can find solace in the truth that He knows us like no one else ever could, and His love for us never wavers.

No matter how it might feel to us, God's Word makes it clear that we never grieve alone. Our faithful Comforter holds vigil at our side through our every heartbreak. He witnesses every single tear (Psalm 56:8).

God alone understands the depth of pain you and I have walked through. We can find the sweetest joy in that truth and in realizing that God really is enough when we're hurting.

Enough understanding.

Enough provision.

Enough comfort and strength.

And that is truly reason to rejoice!

> *For all you face today, God is enough.*

~⃟ Five Minutes in the Word ⃟~

I'm leaping and singing in the circle of your love; you saw
my pain, you disarmed my tormentors, you didn't leave
me in their clutches but gave me room to breathe.

Psalm 31:7–8 THE MESSAGE

Let all who take refuge in you be glad; let them ever
sing for joy. Spread your protection over them, that
those who love your name may rejoice in you.

Psalm 5:11

You are my hiding place; you will protect me from trouble
and surround me with songs of deliverance.

Psalm 32:7

You've kept track of my every toss and turn through the sleepless nights,
each tear entered in your ledger, each ache written in your book.

Psalm 56:8 THE MESSAGE

May your unfailing love be my comfort, according
to your promise to your servant.

Psalm 119:76

Charge It to Me

We have three furry little dogs. Belle and Tink are Bichons, and Maggie is a Yorkie. It's fascinating to watch the relational dynamics between them. Belle is the oldest and Maggie, the baby, loves to take Belle's favorite bone away from her when she's not paying attention. That's when Tink intervenes. She'll grab the bone out of Maggie's mouth and deposit it back at Belle's feet. Belle never seems troubled that the bone disappears or grateful when it returns, but that doesn't deter Tink. She is her sister's advocate!

This kind of advocacy that is so cute in a dog is profoundly moving in the life of the apostle Paul. I'm thinking about the letter he wrote to his friend, Philemon, on behalf of a runaway slave named Onesimus.

We don't know how Onesimus became Philemon's slave or why he ran away from his master, but we do know that he ran straight into the unexpected, life-changing power of

Jesus Christ. And Paul found himself between his friend the master and the slave who had become like a son to him (Philemon v. 10).

Slavery was commonplace in the Roman Empire. Paul could have stuck with the status quo and treated Onesimus as the law and his culture regarded him—one who was property, utterly without rights—but Paul didn't. He chose a different path. He sent Onesimus back home to Philemon with a letter in his hand, one that advocated for Onesimus's protection and freedom.

Roman law gave room for Philemon to punish his runaway slave any way he saw fit, even to the point of death,[9] but Paul boldly asked Philemon to set Onesimus free. Paul pleaded with Philemon to receive Onesimus not as a slave, but as a brother; after all, now slave and master shared a faith in the risen Jesus. Paul even went so far as to tell Philemon that if Onesimus was in debt to him in any way, "Charge it to me" (Philemon v. 18). He volunteered to become personally responsible for someone else's burden.

Paul is a wonderful example of the beauty of extending mercy and kindness to those who are vulnerable. Each time I have done this in my own life, I have found it to be the most joyful of all ministries. After all, it is also profoundly reflective of Christ's heart toward us, isn't it?

Hear Paul's words in 2 Corinthians 5:21: "For our sake [God the Father] made [Jesus] to be sin who knew no sin, so that in him we might become the righteousness of God" (ESV).

Today let's look with eyes of compassion upon those who are vulnerable and hurting. May we, like Paul, be faithful to reflect the great kindness of God and meet them in their places of need.

Find joy in being the hands and feet of Christ today.

⟡ Five Minutes in the Word ⟡

"You shall love the Lord your God with all your heart and with all your soul and with all your mind. This is the great and first commandment. And a second is like it: You shall love your neighbor as yourself. On these two commandments depend all the Law and the Prophets."

Matthew 22:37–40 ESV

Religion that is pure and undefiled before God, the Father,
is this: to visit orphans and widows in their affliction,
and to keep oneself unstained from the world.
James 1:27 ESV

Yes, they shall sing of the ways of the LORD, for great is
the glory of the LORD. Though the LORD is on high, yet He
regards the lowly; but the proud He knows from afar.
Psalm 138:5–6 NKJV

Make sure that nobody pays back wrong for wrong, but always
strive to do what is good for each other and for everyone else.
1 Thessalonians 5:15

Be kind and compassionate to one another, forgiving
each other, just as in Christ God forgave you.
Ephesians 4:32

Our True Home

When was the last time you stopped the business of life for a moment to think about God's promise of heaven? Consider some thoughts from believers who have done just that . . .

The Reverend Billy Graham said, "God will prepare everything for our perfect happiness in heaven, and if it takes my dog being there, I believe he'll be there."[10]

Evangelist D. L. Moody said, "Some day you will read in the papers that D. L. Moody of East Northfield is dead. Don't you believe a word of it! At that moment I shall be more alive than I am now. I shall have gone up higher, that is all, out of this old clay tenement into a house that is immortal—a body that death cannot touch, that sin cannot taint: a body fashioned like unto His glorious body."

What does God Himself say about it?

Heaven is a place where there will be no hunger, no pain, no sickness, no sadness, no reason to fear (Revelation 21:3–4).

It's our true home, where beloved people to whom we have said good-bye will be ready to welcome us (1 Thessalonians 4:13–18).

God's heaven is an eternal kingdom where we will experience infinite peace and joy, and where nothing will stand between us and our Savior (John 14:3).

Near the end of His life, as the heartbreak of the cross grew near, Jesus comforted His disciples with a hint of heaven: "Trust me. There is plenty of room for you in my Father's home. If that weren't so, would I have told you that I'm on my way to get a room ready for you? And if I'm on my way to get your room ready, I'll come back and get you" (John 14:1–3 THE MESSAGE). Could the disciples have received any better news than that?

And it's great news for us too. The trouble and pain we know in this world won't last forever. What will last forever is the future joyful home with our Savior who loves us.

William Barclay offered this perspective: "For the Christian, heaven is where Jesus is. We do not need to speculate on what heaven will be like. It is enough to know that we will be forever with Him."[11]

Jesus has gone to get our rooms ready, and He is returning soon.

Hallelujah!

> *Heaven is far beyond anything we can imagine—*
> *infinitely good, perfect, and soul-satisfying.*

‿⟆ Five Minutes in the Word ⟆‿

Thomas said to [Jesus], "Lord, we do not know where you are going.
How can we know the way?" Jesus said to him, "I am the way, and the
truth, and the life. No one comes to the Father except through me."

John 14:5–6 ESV

I saw a new heaven and a new earth, for the first heaven and the first earth had
passed away, and the sea was no more. And I saw the holy city, new Jerusalem,
coming down out of heaven from God, prepared as a bride adorned for her husband.

Revelation 21:1–2 ESV

He will wipe away every tear from their eyes, and death shall be no more, neither shall
there be mourning, nor crying, nor pain anymore, for the former things have passed away.

Revelation 21:4 ESV

He who testifies to these things says, "Surely I am
coming soon." Amen. Come, Lord, Jesus!

Revelation 22:20 ESV

Jesus answered [the criminal crucified next to Him], "Truly
I tell you, today you will be with me in paradise."

Luke 23:43

Giving with an
Abundance of Joy

When you think of someone who is famous for being generous, who comes to mind? Perhaps it's billionaire philanthropists like Warren Buffet or Bill and Melinda Gates. These people have definitely used their money to do a lot of good, but I've discovered that some of the most remarkably generous people give not out of their wealth, but out of their poverty.

That's what a young Italian woman named Gemma Galgani did. She was born to a middle-class family in the spring of 1878. Her father, a chemist, earned a comfortable living for their family, and he was happy to support Gemma's deep compassion for the needy. Tragically, a series of disasters struck the family, including the death of both of Gemma's parents. Her father's estate was left bankrupt, and Gemma and her siblings found themselves in the same state of crushing poverty as the desperate people young Gemma had helped throughout her youth.[12]

The money was gone, but Gemma's spirit of generosity remained. She continued to give generously to the needy out of her own limited resources. Her aunt once shared a memorable conversation she had with Gemma: "At that time we ourselves were in reduced circumstances, so that I felt compelled to tell her: 'There will be nothing left for our own supper.' Gemma used to answer: 'Providence will give us plenty.'"[13]

Gemma was a living example of the kind of generosity flowing out of poverty that Paul directly linked to an "abundance of joy" in 2 Corinthians 8:2 (ESV). Pointing to the Macedonians as an example of generosity, he said, "In a severe test of affliction, their abundance of joy and their extreme poverty have overflowed into a wealth of generosity on their part."

So how did the Macedonians do it? How did Gemma? What is the secret to this "abundant joy" and the resulting "wealth of generosity" despite real personal need?

I believe both Gemma and the Macedonians were fueled by their unshakable belief in the goodness of God. When we start with a heart of gratitude for the blessings before us, and then move on to the firm belief that God has promised to be faithful to us, we find ourselves free.

Free to love others well . . .

Free to live life with an open hand to the needy . . .

And beautifully free to live in and give out of God's abundant joy.

> *Pour out your love on others, and God will pour out His life in you.*

ᢒᴄ Five Minutes in the Word ᢒᴄ

We want you to know, brothers, about the grace of God that has been given among the churches of Macedonia, for in a severe test of affliction, their abundance of joy and their extreme poverty have overflowed in a wealth of generosity on their part. For they gave according to their means, as I can testify, and beyond their means, of their own accord, begging us earnestly for the favor of taking part in the relief of the saints.

2 Corinthians 8:1–4 ESV

Give generously to them and do so without a grudging heart; then because of this the Lord your God will bless you in all your work and in everything you put your hand to. There will always be poor people in the land. Therefore I command you to be openhanded toward your fellow Israelites who are poor and needy in your land.

Deuteronomy 15:10–11

God loves it when the giver delights in the giving.

2 Corinthians 9:7 THE MESSAGE

*When you are harvesting in your field and you overlook
a sheaf, do not go back to get it. Leave it for the foreigner,
the fatherless and the widow, so that the Lord your
God may bless you in all the work of your hands.*

Deuteronomy 24:19

*God will come to those who are generous and lend
freely, who conduct their affairs with justice.*

Psalm 112:5

Are You Awake?

If you were to share a pot of coffee with a certain elderly gentleman in downtown Dallas, he would tell you that the very sight of rain still brings tears to his eyes.

He is one of many Texans who remember the terrible drought of the 1950s, when it seemed the sky had run dry. It lasted for seven years and left the state in an agonizing water shortage. Crops shriveled and died, creeks became sandpits, and wells dried up. When the rain finally came, the state had been scarred forever.[14]

When I hear stories of hardship like this, it jolts me awake. I suddenly start seeing all kinds of things I've been casually taking for granted.

I turn on a faucet and expect water to run clean and cold.

I see summer leaves turn myriad shades of red, orange, and gold before they surrender to winter's icy blast, knowing that spring will come.

I drive into brilliant sunsets on my route home.

I crunch into juicy apples and sip steaming tea.

All are gifts to celebrate and treasure! When did you last pause to soak in the wonder of it all? The change of the seasons . . . the beauty of the night sky . . . the faithfulness of the harvest . . .

The miraculous is all around us—a truth no one appreciated more fully than the psalmist. Psalm 104 is full of glorious praise exalting our God the King who is "clothed with splendor and majesty" (v. 1 ESV). Our mighty King, the Ruler of all eternity, is also the Sustainer of life. The psalmist took the time to recognize and praise God for the miracles that are so easy to overlook and take for granted, the ones He performs every single day!

"You make springs gush forth in the valleys" (v. 10 ESV).

"The earth is satisfied with the fruit of your work" (v. 13 ESV).

"You cause the grass to grow for the livestock and plants for man to cultivate" (v. 14 ESV).

He uses the moon "to mark the seasons" (v. 19 ESV).

All creatures look to Him for what they need. He opens His hands and provides (vv. 27–28 ESV).

This is the joyful voice of someone marveling at the works of God's hands. For you and me to know that joy, we need to be awake to the wonder of God's power and faithfulness. We have to be willing to pause and take in the awe-inspiring evidence that the King of the universe is working and is *so worthy of praise*.

Psalm 104 is a wonderful reminder that we don't have to wait until Sunday morning to lift our voices in praise to our God. His mercy and grace and outrageous generosity are all around us.

His joy will break into your life when you are awake to the miraculous and praise Him for all He has done!

> *Let the wonder of God's creation*
> *awaken a joyful praise in you.*

❧ Five Minutes in the Word ❧

May the glory of the LORD endure forever; may the LORD rejoice in
his works, who looks on the earth and it trembles, who touches
the mountains and they smoke! I will sing to the LORD as long
as I live; I will sing praise to my God while I have being. May
my meditation be pleasing to him, for I rejoice in the LORD.
Psalm 104:31–34 ESV

You crown the year with your bounty; your wagon
tracks overflow with abundance.
Psalm 65:11 ESV

He covers the sky with clouds; he supplies the earth with rain and makes grass grow on the hills. He provides food for the cattle and for the young ravens when they call.

Psalm 147:8–9

He determines the number of the stars and calls them each by name.

Psalm 147:4

Praise him, sun and moon; praise him, all you shining stars. Praise him, you highest heavens and you waters above the skies. Let them praise the name of the LORD, for at his command they were created.

Psalm 148:3–5

Eternal Joy

The young mother's face is slightly downcast—sorrowful and resigned. She is seated with the body of her son draped across her lap. Her right arm wraps around his back, cradling him. Her left hand is free, palm upturned in surrender.

The woman in the sculpture is Mary. She holds the body of her son, Jesus, after He was removed from the cross.

Beautiful and breathtaking, the *Pietà* is considered one of Michelangelo's greatest masterpieces. The artist carved the marble with such skill that the folds of Mary's robe look like they're falling softly, pooling on the floor like silk instead of stone.

Michelangelo carved the *Pietà* almost six hundred years ago, yet today's visitors to Rome, Italy, can still enjoy every detail of the sculpture, just as Michelangelo's friends did so long ago. Instead of using softer materials that would have been easier to mold, the master sculpture chose a medium that would last the assault of time—white Carrara marble.[15] That's why the *Pieta*'s beauty remains today.

In John 16, we find Jesus talking to His disciples about what will last and what won't. The disciples were grieving as they anticipated Jesus' return to the Father, and Jesus wanted them to know that their grief would be temporary.

But their joy was another matter entirely. Their *joy* would last forever! Jesus said, "Now is your time of grief, but I will see you again and you will rejoice, and no one will take away your joy" (John 16:22).

I'm sure the days before and after Jesus' death felt endless to the disciples. Perhaps there were also similar times in the years that followed Jesus' ascension, when they were suffering for His name, when they felt as if they'd been waiting for His return forever.

But Jesus was faithful to His promise to them. The moment came for each of them when they were escorted into paradise, a place of never-ending joy.

Maybe you are carrying a heavy load of suffering or grief. The road before you may seem endless with sorrow. Hear me, friend. Suffering is real, *but it is a thing of earth and therefore transient . . . temporary.*

Joy, however, flows from Christ and is therefore eternal.

The day will come when even the beautiful *Pietà* crumbles and returns to the earth from which it was carved, and even then, your never-ending, never-fading joy in Christ will remain as fresh as the day He first called you His own.

Joy in Christ is yours . . . forever!

⁓⟶Five Minutes in the Word⟵⁓

His anger lasts only a moment, but his favor lasts a lifetime; weeping
may stay for the night, but rejoicing comes in the morning.

Psalm 30:5

I heard a loud voice from the throne saying, "Look! God's dwelling place
is now among the people, and he will dwell with them. They will be
his people, and God himself will be with them and be their God."

Revelation 21:3

In keeping with his promise we are looking forward to a new
heaven and a new earth, where righteousness dwells.

2 Peter 3:13

The Lord himself will come down from heaven, with a loud command, with the voice
of the archangel and with the trumpet call of God, and the dead in Christ will rise first.

1 Thessalonians 4:16

"If I go and prepare a place for you, I will come back and take
you to be with me that you also may be where I am."

John 14:3

So Many Reasons to Rejoice

This was Bryan Doherty's moment, and it had been four years in the making.

It was late in the fourth quarter. As team manager, Bryan was sitting on the bench just as he had for every basketball game throughout his four years of high school. Suddenly, the coach called his name. In the last game of his senior year, Bryan got a chance to hit the court for the first time ever.

Bryan, who has Down syndrome, ran out to join the other players. Then, as the clock ticked down, a teammate threw him the basketball. Bryan took the shot . . . and it went in!

"The stands roared. It was so loud," his sister Carolyn said. "Everybody was cheering. People on the *other team* were cheering."

"It sounded like everyone was cheering my name," Bryan remembered.[16]

Wow, what an amazing moment! I bet the apostle Paul

would have loved it. I can just imagine him turning to the early church and saying, "See! This is what Christian community should look like. If one of us has a reason to rejoice, *we all* should be filled with the same joy."

Christian community is truly a gift from God. As the body of Christ, we are His hands and His feet; we are His great compassion and love expressed in human form to one another. I can't imagine going through some of the difficult seasons of my life apart from the comfort and encouragement I've received from my Christian friends.

As Paul pointed out in Romans 12, part of what distinguishes us as true believers is that when our brothers or sisters have a reason to rejoice, we rejoice right alongside them. Have you ever thought about the fact that this shared joy is a gift as well? As part of the family of believers, our opportunities for rejoicing are not limited to our own experience—they are endless! If we really practiced this, I think most of us would find it difficult to make it through a single day without abundant reason to rejoice.

Yet the enemy loves for us to be envious when others do well, or to feel as if their success in some way diminishes us. That's not the way God calls His daughters to live.

Instead, let's throw a party when our friends do well! Let's stuff their cars with pink balloons! Cheer them on at full volume! Let's enter into their joy and celebrate God's goodness.

Joy shared is joy increased!

> *Because of Jesus, we are people of joy—so celebrate!*

✺ Five Minutes in the Word ✺

Love one another with brotherly affection.
Outdo one another in showing honor.
Romans 12:10 ESV

Rejoice with those who rejoice, weep with those who weep. Live in harmony
with one another. Do not be haughty, but associate with the lowly.
Romans 12:15–16 ESV

If one part suffers, every part suffers with it; if one part is honored, every part
rejoices with it. Now you are the body of Christ, and each one of you is a part of it.
1 Corinthians 12:26–27

He is the head of the body, the church; he is the beginning
and the firstborn from among the dead, so that in
everything he might have the supremacy.

Colossians 1:18

If you have any encouragement from being united with Christ, if any
comfort from his love, if any common sharing in the Spirit, if any
tenderness and compassion, then make my joy complete by being like-
minded, having the same love, being one in spirit and of one mind.

Philippians 2:1–2

No More Humbug

One holiday season, *A Christmas Carol* was the only Christmas play offered in our town, so Barry and I took our then eight-year-old son to a matinee performance. I tried to prepare Christian for the appearance of the ghosts of Christmas past, present, and future so he wouldn't be afraid.

"I'm not afraid of any old ghosts, Mom!" he said indignantly. "It's just a play—and I'm eight!"

It was a wonderful performance, and as we walked to the car, Barry asked Christian if he'd enjoyed it.

"I did, Dad," he said. "I loved the ghosts too. I just didn't like the hamburger guy until the end."

It took a few moments for us to realize that he was referring to Ebenezer Scrooge and his memorable line, "Bah! Humbug!"

Scrooge is probably the most famously stingy character in all of literature. If you've ever read or seen *A*

Christmas Carol, though, you may have noticed that he wasn't just stingy with his money, but with grace as well.

Scrooge was bitterly critical of everyone—his nephew, his employees, even people going about their business observing the holiday! As a matter of fact, his catchphrase "Bah! Humbug!" has become a universal condemnation. It means "Nonsense!" as in, "All of this Christmas stuff is a bunch of absolute nonsense!"

I have a feeling Ebenezer Scrooge would have gotten along pretty well with the Pharisees of Jesus' day. Almost every time we run into them in the Gospels, they are self-righteous and mean-spirited, doing their best to catch someone—*anyone*—in some transgression of the law. Over and over again they go to ridiculous lengths to try to trick Jesus into making a mistake that would call for His arrest.

I think the Pharisees' strangest moments were when something amazing happened right in front of them. Everyone else in the room was filled with awe and rejoiced . . . but the *Pharisees completely missed it*, because they were so focused on the way someone broke the rules!

It's a sad waste of a life to be a joy-killer. These days I see many modern-day Pharisees perched on social media, just waiting for someone to say something they disagree with so they can pounce. Why would we waste time judging and tearing down people when we could spend our lives looking for ways to bring them joy . . .

Or praying for those who are struggling . . .

Or helping those who are hurting . . .

Or spending time with God in His Word and in prayer?

A critical spirit is a real joy-killer. Today, let's make the most of every opportunity to show people God's beauty and kindness. Let's splash the world with grace, the gift that keeps on giving!

> *Be a blessing—spread grace and joy, not judgment.*

༫ Five Minutes in the Word ༓

Why do you pass judgment on your brother? Or you, why do you despise
your brother? For we will all stand before the judgment seat of God.

Romans 14:10 ESV

"Do not judge, or you too will be judged. For in the same way you judge others, you will be judged, and with the measure you use, it will be measured to you."

Matthew 7:1–2

Let us not pass judgment on one another any longer, but rather decide never to put a stumbling block or hindrance in the way of a brother.

Romans 14:13 ESV

Grow in the grace and knowledge of our Lord and Savior Jesus Christ. To him be glory both now and forever! Amen.

2 Peter 3:18

The grace of God has appeared that offers salvation to all people.

Titus 2:11

Joyful Praise

One of the greatest privileges of my life was the opportunity I had to work with Dr. Billy Graham and his amazing ministry team. For over fifty years, Dr. Graham, Cliff Barrows, and George Beverly Shea (Bev) took the gospel of Jesus Christ around the world. I loved listening to their vast treasury of stories like this one Bev told about his friend Burt Frizen.

As a college student, Burt Frizen was known for his beautiful baritone voice. After he finished his studies, he traded his books and papers for an army uniform and rifle, and he left the safety of home for hostile German soil.

Burt entered combat, and the day that every soldier hopes to avoid arrived: he was badly wounded in battle.

For six hours he lay alone, suffering and sure he was dying. A hymn his mother loved to sing came to his mind, comforted his heart, and eventually reached his weak lips. As hours slipped by, he sang the words over and over:

There is a name to me most dear
Like sweetest music to my ear
For when my heart is troubled, filled with fear,
Jesus whispers peace.

Burt was startled by a movement. A German soldier was approaching him, and Burt was convinced his life was over. Instead, the soldier said, "Sing it again!"

So Burt continued to sing as the soldier slipped his arms beneath him, lifted him from the ground, and then carried him to a stone outcropping where he placed him gently before walking away.

Moments later, U.S. forces found Burt and took him to safety.[17]

What an example Burt offered us! When everything goes wrong, when the disappointments or sufferings are unending, we can choose hope and joy by choosing to worship God. The reason praise is so powerful is that it puts our minds and hearts back in the right place—it lifts them to eternal truths that bring strength, comfort, and great joy. Through praise we remember that we serve a mighty, faithful, and good God who *loves* us.

So on those gray days, lift your voice in praise! Sing through all the worship songs you can remember, and you might even find that something a bit miraculous happens.

Your perspective changes.

Your heart lifts.

Your strength and joy are renewed.

And who knows who might be listening? Such joy can have a wonderful ripple effect!

> **When joy seems impossible,**
> **sing out the goodness of God.**

⟿ Five Minutes in the Word ⟾

Sing to God, sing in praise of his name, extol him who rides on the clouds; rejoice before him—his name is the Lord.

Psalm 68:4

Let everything that has breath praise the Lord. Praise the Lord.

Psalm 150:6

Through Jesus, therefore, let us continually offer to God a sacrifice
of praise—the fruit of lips that openly profess his name.

Hebrews 13:15

I called to the LORD, who is worthy of praise, and
I have been saved from my enemies.

Psalm 18:3

Sing joyfully to the LORD, you righteous; it is
fitting for the upright to praise him.

Psalm 33:1

Don't Miss It!

Have you taken time recently just to look around you? While sitting at a stoplight . . .

Or in a crowd at an airport . . .

Or even at your child's sporting event.

If you do, you might be shocked by what you see: most of us are glued to the little glowing screen in our hands while life goes on all around us. I once saw a series of videos of people actually getting into accidents because they were walking while staring into their phones. People walked into each other and into light poles. One poor woman fell into a manhole, while another walked straight into the fountain at the mall!

Sometimes I get the sinking feeling that we are all so plugged into the vast cyberspace world available to us that we're missing the *real* life that is right in front of us.

Our children are growing up.

The breathtaking beauty of God's creation is on riotous display.

People are smiling at us and doing kind things for one another.

Psalm 90 says, "Teach us to number our days that we may get a heart of wisdom" (v. 12 ESV). The psalmist recognized that life is short and that none of us can predict when ours will end. So he asked God to help him remember this truth and live wisely in light of it.

Surely one aspect of "numbering our days" is embracing the wisdom of living them fully, savoring each moment as the gift that it is, being truly present in whatever we're doing. That may mean putting down our cell phones more often.

On a recent weekend home from college, Christian told us that when he goes out to eat with friends, they all put their phones in the middle of the table. If anyone picks theirs up, they have to pay for everyone's dinner! Not a bad idea, is it?

So put down the screen and look around you. Take time to drink deeply of each and every moment. Life is a beautiful gift. Don't miss the joy!

And besides, do you want two million people seeing the YouTube video of you falling into the fountain at the mall?

> *Find joy in the goodness of God all around you.*

✒ Five Minutes in the Word ✒

Don't waste your time on useless work, mere busywork, the barren
pursuits of darkness. Expose these things for the sham they are. It's
a scandal when people waste their lives on things they must do in
the darkness where no one will see. Rip the cover off those frauds and
see how attractive they look in the light of Christ. Wake up from your
sleep, climb out of your coffins; Christ will show you the light!

Ephesians 5:11–14 THE MESSAGE

My frame was not hidden from you, when I was being made in
secret, intricately woven in the depths of the earth. Your eyes saw my
unformed substance; in your book were written, every one of them, the
days that were formed for me, when as yet there was none of them.

Psalm 139:15–16 ESV

Teach us to number our days, that we may gain a heart of wisdom.

Psalm 90:12

As a father shows compassion to his children, so the LORD shows
compassion to those who fear him. For he knows our frame; he
remembers that we are dust. As for man, his days are like grass; he
flourishes like a flower of the field; for the wind passes over it, and
it is gone, and its place knows it no more. But the steadfast love of
the LORD is from everlasting to everlasting on those who fear him.

Psalm 103:13–17 ESV

Be very careful, then, how you live—not as unwise but as wise,
making the most of every opportunity, because the days are evil.

Ephesians 5:15–16

Come On In

It was a cruise to remember, but not for the reasons you might imagine.

Max Lucado, Sandi Patty, and I were hosting a trip from Boston to the Caribbean. We arrived at the dock just in time to see the crew disembarking and taking all the food with them. Christian addressed the elephant on the dock: "Mom, why are they all leaving and taking the food?"

"It must be a change of crew," I reasoned. "I'm sure our crew will be here any moment with enough food to feed an army."

I was wrong.

Another company had purchased the ship, and although the crew was supposed to work one more week, they'd decided to bolt and take as much stuff as they could carry with them!

So we waited in port for another day while a skeleton staff rustled up more workers and some food. It was not quite what the brochure promised. One evening more than eight hundred passengers lined up to receive one slice of pizza. (I'm sure it was the only seven-day cruise ever where people lost weight!)

But God was at work in the midst of what was not working.

Our group of about three hundred people decided that we would worship and celebrate regardless of our circumstances, and it became clear that true joy—joy in the love of God—is infectious.

When we finally made it to the Bahamas, we held a candlelight service in a small local church. Breaking the bread and passing the wine, we gave thanks that before we even knew the name *Jesus*, He died for our sins so that we can be welcomed into His presence. As we worshipped, other passengers who were not part of our group came in and joined us. We welcomed them with great joy, just as Paul encouraged believers to do (Philippians 2:29).

We are living in challenging times. When we live as those who have hope, joy, and peace because of Christ, people can't help but notice. Who in your neighborhood or workplace needs to know Jesus? Why not invite them to dinner or have a neighborhood party? You don't have to be a gifted evangelist to share your life and your home with others. Just welcome them with joy, and trust the Spirit to make it a time to share the love of God as well.

When we show hospitality to others, we are acting like Jesus, who fed the multitudes and broke the bread and passed the wine at the Last Supper with His disciples. Our Savior also promised to feast with us when we reach our heavenly home, and He told us that He is getting our room ready for the time when we will join Him at last (Revelation 19:9; John 14:2)!

If our heavenly Father has extended such lavish hospitality to us, don't you think we should do the same for others?

> *Put the joy of Jesus on display and welcome others to share in it.*

⮜ Five Minutes in the Word ⮞

We ought therefore to show hospitality to such people so that we may work together for the truth.

3 John v. 8

Share with the Lord's people who are in need. Practice hospitality.

Romans 12:13

Offer hospitality to one another without grumbling. Each of you should use whatever gift you have received to serve others, as faithful stewards of God's grace in its various forms.

1 Peter 4:9–10

"Anyone who gives you a cup of water in my name because you belong to the Messiah will certainly not lose their reward."

Mark 9:41

"The King will reply, 'Truly I tell you, whatever you did for one of the least of these brothers and sisters of mine, you did for me.'"

Matthew 25:40

Cheerful, Hopeful Endurance

The blacksmith placed the iron into the fire. Once it was glowing red-hot, he used his tongs to remove it, and he struck it repeatedly with a hammer. Then . . .

Back into the fire until glowing . . .

Countless blows from the hammer . . .

Only to return to the fire once more.

Fire and hammer, fire and hammer—the blacksmith did this again and again until, at last, his work was complete. From a shapeless piece of iron he had fashioned a perfect horseshoe.

I love this image because it so perfectly captures the work God does to mold our character and make us more like Jesus. That message certainly seems to be what James was communicating in the first few verses of his book.

James wrote to Christians who were going through difficult times, and he had a radical message for them. He told his readers to consider their trials "pure joy" because

the fire of adversity was the very tool God used to forge perseverance in their lives.

Most of us are familiar with the word *perseverance*. Maybe it makes you think of someone who keeps going even when the path gets rough or someone who stays on their diet all the way through the holidays. Both examples do show perseverance, but the Greek gives us a little more insight. In the original language of James 1:3, the word translated *perseverance* means "cheerful, or hopeful endurance; constancy."

It is one thing to keep going no matter what; it is something far more beautiful to do so *cheerfully* and *hopefully*.

Are you going through a hard time today? You can safely trust that even though the fire of adversity is hot, your loving Savior holds you securely in His hand. He will be forever faithful to His work in your heart, endeavoring to bring forth cheerful, hopeful endurance in you.

And that truth, James reminds us, is reason for pure joy.

> *God is with you and for you—He's*
> *making something beautiful in you!*

✑ Five Minutes in the Word ✑

*Consider it pure joy, my brothers and sisters, whenever you face
trials of many kinds, because you know that the testing of your
faith produces perseverance. Let perseverance finish its work so that
you may be mature and complete, not lacking anything.*

James 1:2–4

*He who began a good work in you will bring it to
completion at the day of Jesus Christ.*

Philippians 1:6 ESV

*We ought always to give thanks to God for you, brothers beloved by the Lord,
because God chose you as the firstfruits to be saved, through sanctification
by the Spirit and belief in the truth. To this he called you through our
gospel, so that you may obtain the glory of our Lord Jesus Christ.*

2 Thessalonians 2:13–14 ESV

*Be patient, then, brothers and sisters, until the Lord's coming.
See how the farmer waits for the land to yield its valuable crop,
patiently waiting for the autumn and spring rains.*

James 5:7

Be joyful in hope, patient in affliction, faithful in prayer.

Romans 12:12

Joy in His Presence

There was some serious prime-time drama playing out right before my eyes.

Casey and Rebecca had been separated by thousands of miles for more than two years, and now they were finally reunited. Someone grabbed a video camera to capture the long-awaited reunion as the two friends ran toward each other.

What joy! There were lots of hugs and happy tears and squeals of delight. It was a picture-perfect reunion until . . .

Casey passed out.

Casey, you see, is a miniature schnauzer. He hadn't seen Rebecca, his owner, for the two years she was working in Slovenia. Being in her presence once again was just too much for him. Overwhelmed, he fainted from pure joy. (Don't you just love dogs?)

If a miniature schnauzer can find such happiness in

his owner, how much greater should my joy be in the presence of Jesus!

The psalmist-king David experienced exactly that: "You make known to me the path of life; in your presence there is fullness of joy; at your right hand are pleasures forevermore" (Psalm 16:11 ESV).

You and I can find joy—*immense* joy—in God's presence. The challenge, however, is this: if you're like me, there is a lot competing with God for your attention. We have responsibilities with work and family. Many of us volunteer in our churches and communities. If we ever have any empty space in our lives, we often fill it up with easy-access entertainment. Sometimes there is so much to see and do and be that it's difficult even to get enough sleep.

This kind of busyness has left me, and maybe you, hungry for real joy. Only our heavenly Father and faithful God can pour joy into our lives until we are *full* . . . until we are satisfied.

Why don't you make some room in your life today to rest in God's presence? You may need to turn off a screen, silence your phone, or block out some time on your calendar. There will be some kind of cost involved with this choice, for sure—but I can promise you that any time spent with Him will be so much more than worth it.

In the quiet, you will find that He has been waiting for you all along, and there, in His presence, you will find fullness of joy.

⁓ Five Minutes in the Word ⁓

Rejoice in the Lord always; again I will say, rejoice. Let your
reasonableness be known to everyone. The Lord is at hand.

Philippians 4:4–5 ESV

Blessed are those who have learned to acclaim you, who walk in the light of your
presence, LORD. They rejoice in your name all day long; they celebrate your righteousness.

Psalm 89:15–16

You prepare a table before me in the presence of my enemies.
You anoint my head with oil; my cup overflows.

Psalm 23:5

You have made known to me the paths of life; you
will fill me with joy in your presence.

Acts 2:28

Surely you have granted him unending blessings and
made him glad with the joy of your presence.

Psalm 21:6

Awards Season

I'll never forget my night at the Grammy Awards.

My second record (yes, they were *records* back then) had been nominated for Best Contemporary Christian Album. I didn't think I had much chance of winning (I was prophetic), but I was so excited just to be there. My record company had arranged for a limo to pick me up at my hotel and take me to the Shrine Auditorium in Los Angeles. When the driver pulled up to the red carpet, the world's press ran to see which star would step out. When they saw me, they disappeared faster than half-price televisions on Black Friday.

I didn't care. I was wearing a sparkly dress, and I was going to the Grammys!

It's fun to receive awards for what we do. Giddy kids line up for their plastic, faux-gold trophies at the end of soccer season. Authors, musicians, and scientists list their honors and awards on their websites. Many Americans watch all the entertainment awards shows to see if their favorite artists are chosen. Awards are a big deal.

Jesus thinks rewards are a big deal too. As a matter of fact, He says we should get really excited about them—jump-and-do-cartwheels excited! But the way we store up rewards in heaven is not through winning a game, writing a bestseller, or recording a number one song. Jesus says we will receive great rewards when we serve Him—when we care for the needy, when we share His good news with people who don't know Him, and when we are persecuted for His sake. *Yikes.*

Listen to how *The Message* puts Jesus' teaching in Luke 6:22–23: "Count yourself blessed every time someone cuts you down or throws you out, every time someone smears or blackens your name to discredit me. What it means is that the truth is too close for comfort and that that person is uncomfortable. You can be glad when that happens—skip like a lamb, if you like!—for even though they don't like it, I do . . . and all heaven applauds."

The phrase "skip like a lamb" here also can be translated "leap for joy." The Bible talks about joy quite a lot, but it doesn't often go so far as to say that we have an occasion to "leap for joy."

Our God is faithful and just, and He is incredibly honored when we share in His suffering by bearing the weight of persecution for His sake. If you are going through a difficult time because of your faith in Christ, find strength in this truth: nothing we suffer in the name of Jesus ever goes unnoticed.

Or unrewarded.

> *God's rewards are always worth their cost.*

✤ Five Minutes in the Word ✤

"Whoever finds their life will lose it, and whoever
loses their life for my sake will find it."

Matthew 10:39

"Everyone who has left houses or brothers or sisters of father or
mother or wife or children or fields for my sake will receive a
hundred times as much and will inherit eternal life. But many
who are first will be last, and many who are last will be first."

Matthew 19:29–30

Do not throw away your confidence; it will be richly rewarded. You need to persevere so that when you have done the will of God, you will receive what he has promised.

Hebrews 10:35–36

One thing God has spoken, two things have I heard: "Power belongs to you, God, and with you, Lord, is unfailing love"; and, "You reward everyone according to what they have done."

Psalm 62:11–12

Whoever is kind to the poor lends to the LORD, and he will reward them for what they have done.

Proverbs 19:17

Seeking the Father's Agenda and Joy

Maybe you've heard of Team Hoyt. If you don't know about this father-son duo, then you need to learn about them.

It all began in 1962, when Dick Hoyt and his wife welcomed a baby boy into the world—one with serious health issues. Due to oxygen loss at birth, their son Rick developed cerebral palsy and became a quadriplegic. He would never ride a bike or play baseball or even say his parents' names.

One day, when Rick was thirteen years old, he communicated a surprising request to his dad through his computer. He wanted to participate in a five-mile run to raise money for a young man who had been paralyzed in an accident. Although his father was no runner, he agreed to run and push his son in the wheelchair.

They ran the race and came in dead last, but that night at home Rick told his dad, "When I'm running, it feels like I'm not handicapped." That was all it took to set the father and son on a whole new, lifelong trajectory.

Since that run in 1977, Dick Hoyt has pushed his son in over one thousand races, including six Ironman championships. He has run behind Rick, swum while pulling him in a dinghy, and pedaled a bike with Rick sitting on a special seat on the handlebars.[18]

Once someone suggested Dick try one race without his boy. "No way," he said.[19]

Clearly Dick Hoyt didn't compete for the thrill of the race. He sacrificed himself for the love of his son. He spent his energy bringing joy to his son, and then he shared in his son's joy.

I think this is a pretty good picture of why Paul was filled with joy even while chained to a burly guard in a Roman prison. In his letter to the Philippians, he assured his readers that, though his circumstances were difficult, there was only one thing that mattered to him: that the gospel of Jesus Christ was preached. If that happened, then Paul was carrying out the Father's agenda—he was putting his love for his heavenly Father into action and bringing Him joy. If that happened, then Paul himself had reason to rejoice.

When we are focused on our own temporal desires, we become frustrated because we can't control how our circumstances unfold. But the moment we let go of our own agenda and seek God's priorities instead, we find ourselves part of something far more beautiful than we ever could have imagined. We are part of something *eternal* . . . the works of the great God of the universe. And we are caught up in things that bring His heart joy.

Then, with Paul, we can confidently say, "Yes, and I will rejoice" (Philippians 1:18 ESV).

> *God has a joy-producing role*
> *for you in His agenda today.*

∼⟨~ Five Minutes in the Word ∼⟩~

"Seek first the kingdom of God and his righteousness,
and all these things will be added to you."
Matthew 6:33 ESV

Some indeed preach Christ from envy and rivalry, but others from good will. The latter do it out of love, knowing that I am put here for the defense of the gospel. The former proclaim Christ out of selfish ambition, not sincerely but thinking to afflict me in my imprisonment. What then? Only that in every way, whether in pretense or in truth, Christ is proclaimed, and in that I rejoice. Yes, and I will rejoice.

Philippians 1:15–18 ESV

Whatever you do, work heartily, as for the Lord and not for men, knowing that from the Lord you will receive the inheritance as your reward. You are serving the Lord Christ.

Colossians 3:23–24 ESV

"Store up for yourselves treasures in heaven, where moths and vermin do not destroy, and where thieves do not break in and steal. For where your treasure is, there your heart will be also."

Matthew 6:20–21

We remember before our God and Father your work produced by faith, your labor prompted by love, and your endurance inspired by hope in our Lord Jesus Christ.

1 Thessalonians 1:3

A Joyful Ending

Have you ever prayed for something for so long that one day you found you no longer had the faith to believe God would come through for you?

I think it's a pretty safe bet that's exactly where Zechariah was when the angel Gabriel showed up. He and his wife, Elizabeth, had longed for a child for many years—decades actually. Undoubtedly, Zechariah and Elizabeth had offered countless prayers to God, asking Him to bless them with a child, but the years slipped by with no answer. Elizabeth remained barren until the couple grew too old to hold out hope any longer.

Zechariah had so thoroughly lost faith that God would answer his prayer for a child that he didn't believe God's yes when it finally came . . . *even though the message was delivered by the angel Gabriel!*

In addition to its happy ending, do you know what I really like about this story? Zechariah's complete loss of faith didn't hinder God's response to his prayer.

Elizabeth still conceived. Zechariah still had the joy of holding his infant son in his aged and weathered hands.

So why is it so hard for us to imagine that God might understand when we hit a point at which our faith has worn thin and our hearts are weary?

The prodigal hasn't returned. If anything, he's walked farther away.

The cancer has been in remission more than once, and now it has returned yet again.

It's been years of many interviews; not one job offer. Savings are almost gone.

Paperwork and who-knows-what keep the adopted child in Africa instead of in the bedroom awaiting her.

Zechariah and Elizabeth's story shows us that God's great power is not hindered by our weakness. He is more than able to meet us in our most desperate longings, whether or not our one-thousandth prayer is filled with the same zealous faith as the first.

After Gabriel told Zechariah that Elizabeth would have a son, this divine messenger also said that Zechariah himself would "have joy and gladness, and many will rejoice at his birth" (Luke 1:14 ESV).

Then, in Luke 1:58, we find Elizabeth holding a baby boy named John. Scripture tells us, "Her neighbors and relatives heard that the Lord had shown great mercy to her, and they rejoiced with her" (ESV).

However weary you may be today from a long-aching heart, remember this: our God is a kind and gracious Father who bends His ear low to hear our cry. He knows your heart. He is right there with you. He loves you, His dear daughter.

And His boundless goodness may just take you by surprise down the road. Who knows what joyful endings may be around the bend?

> *Rejoice that God's great power is*
> *not hindered by our weakness!*

◦⟨ Five Minutes in the Word ⟩◦

The LORD has heard my cry for mercy; the LORD accepts my prayer.

Psalm 6:9

I love the LORD, for he heard my voice; he heard my cry for mercy.

Psalm 116:1

All my longings lie open before you, Lord; my
sighing is not hidden from you.

Psalm 38:9

Hope deferred makes the heart sick, but a longing fulfilled is a tree of life.

Proverbs 13:12

May my prayer be set before you like incense; may the
lifting up of my hands be like the evening sacrifice.

Psalm 141:2

The Gift of Forgiveness

W hat are the odds?

"That's my daughter! That's my daughter, Wanda!" Victor Peraza could be heard exclaiming as a nurse ran sobbing from his hospital room. He had not seen Wanda since the day he had walked out on his family forty-one years earlier when she was a baby. Now a cancer patient facing his final days, Victor had met his daughter.

When Wanda first heard the name of this man who had been admitted to the hospital, she had to see if he was the father she'd never known. One look into the green eyes—a mirror image of her own—reflected the truth: he was her father. Overwhelmed, she ran from the room in tears.

During the few days Wanda and her dad had before he passed, she spent every moment she could with him. She told him she loved him, and she introduced him to her children.

Wanda could have refused to allow her dad back into her life, but she chose forgiveness instead. Her reward was

extraordinary joy. "I feel blessed," she told a journalist who marveled at her ability to forgive and the obvious joy that resulted.[20]

As Christians, most of us know that God commands us to forgive. Scripture certainly has a lot to say on the subject, and some of the most challenging teachings came from Jesus Himself. He countered His culture's limits on forgiveness by encouraging His disciples to forgive abundantly. He lived out His teachings, forgiving—even as He hung from the cross—the very men who had put Him there.

Yes, we all know we *should* forgive, but what we may not stop to realize on the front end of forgiveness is that there are times, like in Wanda's life, when it holds great gifts. Forgiveness can bring joy to the forgiven as well as the forgiver. It can also bring . . .

The gift of freedom . . .

The gift of a peace-filled heart . . .

The gift of a relationship restored.

Of course, extending forgiveness does not always restore the relationship. Some people we need to forgive are not able or willing to treat us respectfully, and they're simply not safe for us to be around.

But some relationships are able to be restored. God's grace can empower us to forgive and then rebuild. The only way to know that gift of joy waiting for us on the other side of forgiveness is to give it a try.

It would be sad to miss out on a joy like Wanda's, wouldn't it?

> *Forgiveness is God's pathway*
> *to joy in an unfair world.*

✦ Five Minutes in the Word ✦

Put on then, as God's chosen ones, holy and beloved, compassionate hearts, kindness, humility, meekness, and patience, bearing with one another and, if one has a complaint against another, forgiving each other; as the Lord has forgiven you, so you also must forgive.

Colossians 3:12–13 ESV

"Pay attention to yourselves! If your brother sins, rebuke him, and if he repents, forgive him, and if he sins against you seven times in the day, and turns to you seven times, saying 'I repent,' you must forgive him."

Luke 17:3–4 ESV

I therefore, a prisoner for the Lord, urge you to walk in a manner worthy of the calling to which you have been called, with all humility and gentleness, with patience, bearing with one another in love, eager to maintain the unity of the Spirit in the bond of peace.

Ephesians 4:1–3 ESV

He forgave us all our sins, having canceled the charge of our legal indebtedness, which stood against us and condemned us; he has taken it away, nailing it to the cross.

Colossians 2:13–14

Be kind to one another, tenderhearted, forgiving one other, as God in Christ forgave you.

Ephesians 4:32 ESV

A Good Word

It had been a long trip. I first spoke at a women's conference in Hartford, Connecticut. From there I flew through Chicago to Winnipeg, Canada, to record two television shows. The following morning I flew to Toronto for two more television interviews and then recorded ten teaching sessions. Flying home to Dallas, I was squished in the middle seat between two large men who looked as miserable as I felt. Finally I picked up my car and drove home.

When I walked through the door, three happy dogs greeted me with wagging tails, and my husband gave me a big hug. As I put on the kettle to make some tea, Barry innocently asked if I would be able to go with him to take the dogs to the groomer the following morning.

Well, let me just say this: God was not glorified by my response! I had to apologize to Barry, to the Lord, and even to the three dogs. Have you ever been there? Something flew out of your mouth and afterward you were a little horrified. *Did I really say that?* I've had more of these moments than I care to think about.

If you ever want a lesson in humility, take a moment to look up how much the Bible has to say about our tongues . . . the topic comes up more than a few times. But before you cringe and turn away, let me assure you that not all of it is negative. Check out Proverbs 15:23, for instance: "A person finds joy in giving an apt reply—and how good is a timely word!"

Ah . . . so it *is* possible to say the right thing at the right time, what the writer of Proverbs here calls "an apt reply." But what is the secret to getting there?

An apt reply is intentional and thoughtful. Since most of us don't have the ability to deliver that off the cuff, we need to seek God's guidance so that our negative emotions don't rule us. God can teach us and transform us so that we choose life-giving words, whatever the circumstances.

Most of the words I have regretted in my life were spoken in exhaustion, anger, or fear. I tend not to regret my words, though, when I give God time to speak to me before I speak to others. The words He chooses are often very different from the ones I would have chosen in the heat of the moment.

So, the next time you find your emotions running high and your energy tank on empty, remember that you almost never need to respond right away. You can walk away for a while, take a time-out, and give God a chance to speak to you before you speak to someone else. Odds are that when you do, you'll find yourself experiencing the joy that comes with "giving an apt reply."

Weigh your words so they don't weigh others down.

✎ Five Minutes in the Word ✎

Sin is not ended by multiplying words, but the prudent hold their tongues.

Proverbs 10:19

Whoever derides their neighbor has no sense, but the
one who has understanding holds their tongue.

Proverbs 11:12

The words of the reckless pierce like swords, but
the tongue of the wise brings healing.

Proverbs 12:18

The tongue has the power of life and death, and
those who love it will eat its fruit.

Proverbs 18:21

A word fitly spoken is like apples of gold in a setting of silver.

Proverbs 25:11 ESV

Joy with the Trouble

In the summer of 2015, author Bo Stern lost her husband, Steve, after his long, brutal battle with ALS. For many months, she had been his constant caregiver, doing all she could, both day and night, to ease his suffering. It was an exhausting, heartrending labor of love. Then the day she had long expected, but couldn't possibly prepare for, arrived: Steve slipped away to his ultimate healing in Christ. Although Bo and her kids were so happy for him to be free of his suffering at last, the ache of losing him was profound.

But Bo knew a powerful secret: God is never nearer to His children than in times of sorrow.

"I'm not looking to be free of grief," she wrote on her blog. "I think the Bible is clear that sorrow tethers us to the presence of God in a way that few other things can."[21]

The apostle Paul knew of that bittersweet union of sorrow and joy that we experience when we lean into God during times of loss and pain. He wrote to believers who also knew about that union: "You received the word in much affliction, with the joy of the Holy Spirit" (1 Thessalonians 1:6 ESV).

To really grasp the beauty of this verse, we need to look into the original language. The word *affliction* can also be translated "anguish," but the real power for me is in the simple word *with*. It means "accompaniment."

An accompaniment . . . as a pianist provides a mezzo-soprano.

An accompaniment . . . as one gourmet dish enhances the flavor of another.

By the power of the Holy Spirit, joy and sorrow do go hand in hand. This is how Eugene Peterson put it in *The Message*: "Although great trouble accompanied the Word, you were able to take great joy from the Holy Spirit!—taking the trouble with the joy, the joy with the trouble" (1 Thessalonians 1:6).

Because God has given us the precious gift of His Spirit, we are never left destitute in our pain. He gives us the gift of joy in the midst of our sorrow.

> *Joy and sorrow walk hand in hand,*
> *leading us closer to the heart of God.*

⸝ℰ Five Minutes in the Word ℯ⸝

*"I will ask the Father, and he will give you another advocate
to help you and be with you forever—the Spirit of truth."*

John 14:16–17

*Again Jesus said [to his disciples], "Peace be with you! As
the Father has sent me, I am sending you." And with that he
breathed on them and said, "Receive the Holy Spirit."*

John 20:21–22

*Hope does not put us to shame, because God's love has been poured
out into our hearts by the Holy Spirit, who has been given to us.*

Romans 5:5

*Praise be to the God and Father of our Lord Jesus Christ,
the Father of compassion and the God of all comfort.*

2 Corinthians 1:3

*Our gospel came to you not only in word, but also in power and
in the Holy Spirit and with full conviction. . . . You received the
word in much affliction, with the joy of the Holy Spirit.*

1 Thessalonians 1:5–6 ESV

Resting in a Perfect Love

Did you see the video that made the rounds in 2015 of a twelve-year-old Taiwanese boy in a museum? The security footage shows him walking near a guard railing in front of a $1.5 million painting. Just as he passed the masterpiece, he somehow tripped, lost his balance, and started to fall. Instinctively he put out his hand to brace himself and . . . yep, you guessed it! He punched a hole right through the painting.

The final frame of the video shows the horror on the boy's face as he looks around to see who witnessed his million-dollar disaster.[22] I cringed as I watched—I so felt his pain. I have made a career out of tripping over and falling into things.

In reality, that awful mishap is a picture of what it means to be human. We trip. We fall. We break stuff. We say the most outrageous things at the worst possible moments. We run into each other. We forget the very things we are trying the hardest to remember.

And that's actually okay—just as long as we have the humility to *accept* our flaws, weaknesses, and limitations.

Merriam-Webster defines *humility* as "the quality or state of not thinking you are better than other people."[23] The opposite of humility is pretension. You know what that looks like, don't you? *Pretension* is "the unpleasant quality of people who think of themselves as more impressive, successful, or important than they really are."[24]

Pretension is pretending; it is an attempt to display false perfection. It is a weary, soul-dry place to be.

Humility, on the other hand, has made peace with imperfection. Humility doesn't have to display anything; it can just *be.* Humility is free to love well and therefore to live fully, deeply, and joyfully.

Accepting our flaws and weaknesses is risky, difficult territory for most of us. Whenever we blow it, we, like the boy in the video, instinctively look around to see who's watching. Who will judge us? Who will mock us in our failings?

The only way I know to make peace with my imperfections and embrace humility is to rest in the eternal truth that God loves me, *all* of me—trips, falls, and failures included. He loves the imperfect me—and the imperfect you—so perfectly. And what joy there is in the freedom that comes with His love!

> *Dare to be who God created you to be today, for you are fiercely loved!*

҉ Five Minutes in the Word ҉

Let each of you look not only to his own interests, but also to the interests of others. Have this mind among yourselves, which is yours in Christ Jesus, who, though he was in the form of God, did not count equality with God a thing to be grasped, but emptied himself, by taking the form of a servant, being born in the likeness of men.

Philippians 2:4–7 ESV

Before destruction a man's heart is haughty, but humility comes before honor.

Proverbs 18:12 ESV

Good and upright is the LORD; therefore he instructs sinners in the way. He leads the humble in what is right, and teaches the humble his way.

Psalm 25:8–9 ESV

When pride comes, then comes disgrace, but with humility comes wisdom.

Proverbs 11:2

Humble yourselves, therefore, under God's mighty hand, that he may lift you up in due time.

1 Peter 5:6

The Breaking of the Curse

Maybe you know about Narnia, the setting of C. S. Lewis's *The Lion, The Witch, and the Wardrobe*, where an evil queen's curse keeps the land in an endless winter. If you do, you probably also know about the dramatic moment when this frozen world begins to thaw and the signs of spring—signs that the curse had been broken—miraculously appear. First, there are the sounds of moving water as streams and rivers unfreeze. Then snow slides from pine tree branches, and the first spot of green breaks through the landscape of white. Finally, birds begin to sing, and flowers push their way up through the muddy ground.

In a place where everything had felt bare, dead, and gloomy for years . . . *life* arrived.[25]

I can't imagine a better picture of the ministry of Christ. When John the Baptist sent his disciples to ask Jesus whether He was the Messiah, Jesus pointed to the miraculous signs of life surrounding Him: "Go back and tell John what you have just seen and heard: The blind see, the lame walk, lepers are cleansed, the deaf hear, the dead are raised, the wretched of the earth have God's salvation hospitality extended to them" (Luke 7:22 THE MESSAGE).

Yes, indeed . . . He was the One they'd been waiting for.

With every step Jesus took in the desert of Palestine, He was at last breaking Eden's long curse. As the prophets had spoken centuries earlier, this long-awaited Messiah healed the diseased, delivered the demon possessed, comforted the hurting, and freed the oppressed. As N. T. Wright said, "This is what it looks like when God is in charge."[26]

Today our God continues to be in charge. The end of the curse's power draws near, and it's only a matter of time until our victorious King returns and makes all things right. We'll all struggle from time to time as we wait, but we can find joy even in the difficult seasons by recognizing and celebrating all the ways we see the curse breaking.

What signs of His life and beauty surround you today?

> *Rejoice! No matter how troubling things may be, our good King is in charge.*

❧ Five Minutes in the Word ❧

He will judge between the nations and will settle disputes for many peoples. They will beat their swords into plowshares and their spears into pruning hooks. Nation will not take up sword against nation, nor will they train for war anymore.

Isaiah 2:4

"Proclaim this message: 'The kingdom of heaven has come near.' Heal the sick, raise the dead, cleanse those who have leprosy, drive out demons. Freely you have received, freely give."

Matthew 10:7–8

After John was put in prison, Jesus went into Galilee, proclaiming the good news of God. "The time has come," he said. "The kingdom of God has come near. Repent and believe the good news!"

Mark 1:14–15

"The Spirit of the Lord is on me, because he has anointed me to proclaim good news to the poor. He has sent me to proclaim freedom for prisoners and recovery of sight for the blind, to set the oppressed free, to proclaim the year of the Lord's favor."

Luke 4:18–19

Great crowds came to him, bringing the lame, the blind, the crippled, the mute and many others, and laid them at his feet; and he healed them.

Matthew 15:30

The Safest Place
in the World

I had just finished teaching about God's faithfulness when she walked toward me. It took her a few moments to gather herself enough to be able to speak.

"It's my daughter," she said. "We raised her in the church, but she wandered away and is living with her boyfriend. I'm so worried about her."

As women, we love deeply. Sometimes that love is accompanied by some pretty intense anxiety.

God certainly wants us to love well, but He never intended for anxiety to accompany that love. How can we keep it from creeping in?

I think we can find a hint by looking at the way Paul loved those he pastored. He had *a lot* of fragile believers in his circle of love and concern, and it's pretty obvious he felt a fatherly responsibility for them. Yet when he wrote to the

Philippians about their faith journey, he was not filled with hand-wringing anxiety, but with joy.

Let's take a peek at his letter to the Philippians to see if we can discover his secret: "In all my prayers for all of you, I always pray with joy because of your partnership in the gospel from the first day until now, being confident of this, that he who began a good work in you will carry it on to completion until the day of Christ Jesus" (1:4–6).

Did you spot it? Where does Paul place his confidence? And what is the source of his joy?

Paul had great confidence about the Philippians' future, not because they were exceptional Christ followers, but because they were following a faithful God! Paul was confident that the same God who called them to new life in Christ would continue to be at work in them throughout their lives.

Stop for a moment and think about the person you've been most anxious about.

What if you really entrusted that person to God, believing that His care is perfect? Imagine how that would open up space in your heart for joy . . . the joy of anticipating God's good work in the lives of those you love and the joy of what His good work will mean for them. I don't think that kind of focus on God's faithfulness and great love would leave any room for worry, do you?

The people we love are on God's schedule, not ours, and He is good and powerful. He is faithful and true. So may we release them into God's loving hands, remembering that's the safest place in the world for them.

With our hearts freed from worry, who knows how much joy God might bring?

> *Place those you love in the Father's hands . . . it's the safest place there is.*

✒ Five Minutes in the Word ✒

Of this gospel I was appointed a herald and an apostle and a teacher.
That is why I am suffering as I am. Yet this is no cause for shame,
because I know whom I have believed, and am convinced that he
is able to guard what I have entrusted to him until that day.

2 Timothy 1:11–12

We know that anyone born of God does not continue to sin; the One who
was born of God keeps them safe, and the evil one cannot harm them.

1 John 5:18

I planted the seed, Apollos watered it, but God has been making it grow. So neither the one who plants nor the one who waters is anything, but only God, who makes things grow.

1 Corinthians 3:6–7

You also were included in Christ when you heard the message of truth, the gospel of your salvation. When you believed, you were marked in him with a seal, the promised Holy Spirit, who is a deposit guaranteeing our inheritance until the redemption of those who are God's possession—to the praise of his glory.

Ephesians 1:13–14

Fear of man will prove to be a snare, but whoever trusts in the LORD is kept safe.

Proverbs 29:25

Joyful Service

Mother Teresa.

Oskar Schindler.

Clara Barton.

Do you recognize these three names? They are heroes not because they were brilliant or outrageously successful in the world's eyes but because they lived lives of compassion. They lavishly poured out their lives for people who had nothing to offer them in return.

A selfless nun serving in the slums of India, a German businessman who kept hundreds of Jews out of Nazi death camps, and a nurse who founded the Red Cross . . . three remarkable human beings who exemplify extraordinary service to others, often at great personal cost.

But consider what Rabindranath Tagore, the 1913 Nobel Laureate for Literature, wrote: "I slept and dreamt that life was joy. I awoke and saw that life was service. I acted and behold, service was joy."[27]

Perhaps it seems contradictory at first that service and joy should be so closely linked. Wouldn't it make more sense that the most joyful people on earth were the ones who earned well, invested wisely, achieved their dreams, and then sat down in their recliners?

God, however, calls the citizens of His kingdom to live differently. He commissions us to love one another and be kind and compassionate to one another. He challenges us to live our lives in radical service to our neighbors . . .

And that is exactly what Jesus modeled for us.

The Gospels reveal our Messiah to be a very unusual King of kings. Instead of commandeering servants, He became servant to all. He washed His disciples' feet, healed the sick, touched the untouchables, made time for the inconvenient, fed the hungry, and held babies on His lap! Over and over, Scripture tells us He had "compassion" for the people whose paths crossed His (Matthew 9:36; 14:14; 15:32; 20:34). When we open our hearts and hands, our calendars and our checkbooks to those who are suffering, we are following our Redeemer's example.

I love how Paul put it in Ephesians: "Watch what God does, and then you do it, like children who learn proper behavior from their parents. Mostly what God does is love you. Keep company with him and learn a life of love. Observe how Christ loved us. His love was not cautious but extravagant" (5:1–2 THE MESSAGE).

When we serve as Jesus served, we are fulfilling our very destinies as children of God. Is it any wonder that in doing so, we find our hearts filled with joy?

> *May the world see us as filled to overflowing with the love of God.*

⁓&ᴇ Five Minutes in the Word ᴅ⁓

Above all, love each other deeply, because love covers over a multitude of sins.

1 Peter 4:8

Jesus replied: "'Love the Lord your God with all your heart and with all your soul and with all your mind.' This is the first and greatest commandment. And the second is like it: 'Love your neighbor as yourself.' All the Law and the Prophets hang on these two commandments."

Matthew 22:37–40

Command them to do good, to be rich in good deeds,
and to be generous and willing to share.

1 Timothy 6:18

"Then the righteous will answer him, 'Lord, when did
we see you hungry and feed you, or thirsty and give you
something to drink? When did we see you a stranger and
invite you in, or needing clothes and clothe you? When
did we see you sick or in prison and go visit you?'
"The King will reply, 'Truly I tell you, whatever you did for one of
the least of these brothers and sisters of mine, you did for me.'"

Matthew 25:37–40

As we have opportunity, let us do good to all people,
especially to those who belong to the family of believers.

Galatians 6:10

A Child's Eyes

I remember a very windy day when Christian was about five years old. We were walking to our car from the grocery store, and my biggest concern was getting him into his car seat before he blew away.

Suddenly he stopped dead in his tracks. I looked down to see if everything was okay and saw that he was mesmerized by the wind moving the tree branches.

"Look, Mommy! The trees are clapping!" I saw an inconvenience, but Christian saw nature applauding the Creator.

Have you ever watched a young child notice the simplest of things?

The rough texture of a pinecone.

A bird's feather hiding in the grass.

An acorn nestled against the base of an oak tree.

Children often see things that we adults are too busy to notice.

You know, I think children have it right. We are the ones who are missing out. Our world truly *is* full of the miraculous, of remarkable details and *wondrous* moments that have the power to fill our hearts with joy if we simply train our eyes to become childlike again.

The fingerprints of God and His grace are everywhere.

Paul knew this truth, and he used it to argue for the existence of the living God.

He was in a predominantly Gentile city, and he healed a man. The people in the crowd were so amazed that they thought Paul and his friend Barnabas were gods! Chaos broke out because the crowd wanted to offer sacrifices to the two men, who were appalled. Only the one true God deserves such praise!

Paul needed a good argument to point the mob in the right direction for worship. He looked around him and found all the evidence he needed, then said, "[The one true God] has not left himself without testimony: He has shown kindness by giving you rain from heaven and crops in their seasons; he provides you with plenty of food and fills your hearts with joy" (Acts 14:17).

It's easy to be like the crazed crowd in Acts, overlooking countless evidences of God's goodness and grace . . . miracles that a child would never miss.

Today I'm going to put on a new set of lenses, the eyes of a child.

I'll be on the lookout for God's amazing gifts just waiting to be discovered and celebrated.

> *Holy Spirit, open our eyes to*
> *the proof of Your presence.*

❧ Five Minutes in the Word ☙

When I consider your heavens, the work of your fingers, the moon
and the stars, which you have set in place, what is mankind that
you are mindful of them, human beings that you care for them?
Psalm 8:3–4

How many are your works, LORD! In wisdom you made
them all; the earth is full of your creatures.
Psalm 104:24

The LORD builds up Jerusalem; he gathers the exiles of Israel. He
heals the brokenhearted and binds up their wounds. He determines
the number of the stars and calls them each by name.
Psalm 147:2–4

*May the glory of the L*ORD *endure forever; may the L*ORD *rejoice in his works—he who looks at the earth, and it trembles, who touches the mountains, and they smoke. I will sing to the L*ORD *all my life; I will sing praise to my God as long as I live.*

Psalm 104:31–33

God saw all that he had made, and it was very good. And there was evening, and there was morning—the sixth day.

Genesis 1:31

Jam-Packed with His Joy

Countless times each week, believers whisper the words of greatest comfort that we are capable of offering to each other: "I am praying for you."

In times of grief, longing, and suffering, when there are no easy answers, and when our most sincere encouragements would fall short, those five words can bring comfort, strength, and hope for the new day.

Jesus understood this truth. That is one reason why, near the end of His life, He prayed at length for His disciples while He was still with them. Imagine Jesus Himself praying for you!

Often in the Gospels we read that Jesus went away to a quiet place to be alone with the Father and pray, but this time was different. He must have known that a public prayer would provide His disciples with strength, comfort, and joy for months and even years to come. So before He returned to His Father, Jesus asked God to bless and protect His followers. He wanted these faithful ones to know that, even though He would be away from them physically, His love and concern for them would never, ever waver.

"I am coming to you now," Jesus prayed, "but I say these things while I am still in the world, so that [these disciples] may have the full measure of my joy within them" (John 17:13).

I absolutely love the original language here. The phrase translated so politely in the NIV as "the full measure" means "to cram." Jesus wanted His disciples to be completely jam-packed with *His* joy . . . every nook and cranny.

Now, I have the most wonderful news for you: Jesus included you and me in His prayer! Verse 20 says clearly, "My prayer is not for them [the disciples present with Him] alone. I pray also for those who will believe in me through their message." That would be you and me!

Maybe you, like the disciples, have recently received news that broke your heart or left you worried about the future. Be encouraged, my friend! Jesus has returned to the Father, but His love and care for you is ever present. As Hebrews 7:25 says, Jesus is "always on the job to speak up" for us (THE MESSAGE).

Just as He prayed for you in the Upper Room, Jesus prays for you now from heaven above!

> *The Son of the Most High God prays that*
> *you will be full—crammed full—of His joy.*

⤫ Five Minutes in the Word ⤬

Jesus' priesthood is permanent. He's there from now to eternity to save everyone
who comes to God through him, always on the job to speak up for them.

Hebrews 7:24–25 THE MESSAGE

"I will remain in the world no longer, but they are still in the world, and
I am coming to you, Holy Father, protect them by the power of your name,
the name you gave me, so that they may be one as we are one."

John 17:11

The LORD appeared to us in the past, saying: "I have loved you with an
everlasting love; I have drawn you with unfailing kindness."

Jeremiah 31:3

Since we have a great priest over the house of God, let us draw near to God with a
sincere heart and with the full assurance that faith brings, having our hearts sprinkled
to cleanse us from a guilty conscience and having our bodies washed with pure water.

Hebrews 10:21–22

The Spirit helps us in our weakness. We do not know what we ought to pray
for, but the Spirit himself intercedes for us through wordless groans.

Romans 8:26

Contagious Joy

Every weekend in Franklin, Tennessee, kids are on the lookout for a particular police officer. Sometimes on Saturday mornings they spot him at the farmers' market or the soccer complex. On Sundays they may see him directing traffic at a local church.

"There he is!" they shout from backseats and booster seats. "We love that guy!"

Hardly an ordinary traffic officer, this gentleman is a local celebrity.

He is David Collins, "The Dancing Cop."

He stands tall and proud in the middle of the street. His uniform is perfectly accessorized with a reflective vest, a pair of sunglasses, and small earbuds playing his favorite dancing tunes (mostly Elvis). He directs traffic . . . and dances while he does it.

"It is my way of giving something back to the community," Officer Collins says. "I'm trying to bring some happiness, some *joy*, some worship to what I do."[28] He has been bringing smiles while keeping traffic moving smoothly in Franklin for the past six years.

Officer Collins has discovered an important truth about the work we do on this earth: when we view our work as an act of praise to our Creator, that work becomes a powerful source of joy in our lives. What's more . . . it's a *contagious* joy.

You may not have a dancing traffic cop in your neighborhood, but I bet you can think of someone in your world who radiates joy in their work. I've known several people like that, and you know what? None of them had especially exciting jobs.

One man was in charge of bringing shopping carts in the grocery parking lot back into the store.

Another woman swept floors at Costco.

Still another woman worked the drive-through window at my local coffee house.

These people were followers of Christ who made the conscious decision to honor God as they did their work. The joy that overflowed from that decision was positively infectious.

No matter what your work situation is today, it matters to God. He has chosen you to live in this moment, in *this* place, to be His light in a dark world. Offer your work as an act of praise to Him today. Sow seeds of contagious joy!

> *Let's make our work worship
> and flood our world with joy!*

✒ Five Minutes in the Word ✒

*Let the favor of the Lord our God be upon us, and establish the work
of our hands upon us; yes, establish the work of our hands!*
Psalm 90:17 ESV

*Whatever you do, work at it with all your heart, as
working for the Lord, not for human masters, since you
know that you will receive an inheritance from the Lord
as a reward. It is the Lord Christ you are serving.*
Colossians 3:23–24

Whether you eat or drink or whatever you do, do it all for the glory of God.

1 Corinthians 10:31

Since you call on a Father who judges each person's work impartially, live out your time as foreigners here in reverent fear.

1 Peter 1:17

God is not unjust; he will not forget your work and the love you have shown him as you have helped his people and continue to help them.

Hebrews 6:10

The Rights of Citizenship

I'll never forget the day I became an American citizen. It was one of the most joy-filled, profoundly moving days of my life. And the journey to that momentous occasion began with a bad, made-for-television movie! I'll explain . . .

Christian was two years old and tucked up fast asleep in bed when Barry and I turned on the television that evening. I don't remember the title of the movie, but it was about a plane being hijacked. Instead of arriving in Paris, the plane landed on a small airstrip somewhere in the Middle East, and the first thing the hijackers did was separate those with American passports from everyone else onboard. That's all it took. I began applying for citizenship the next day! If Christian and I were ever hijacked, I wanted us to be ushered straight to the same group of people who could prove they were American citizens. If we were going down, we were going down together!

On the day I was sworn in as a citizen, I could hardly

say the words of the oath as tears poured down my cheeks. I thought about all the men, women, and children throughout the years who fought hard and made huge sacrifices to protect this great nation and call it home. I didn't enter into such an honor and a privilege lightly.

The first time I returned from Europe as an American citizen, the passport control officer said, "Welcome home, ma'am." I boohooed again!

One of the things I learned along the way is that there are both certain rights and responsibilities that go along with becoming an American citizen. The same is true for our citizenship in the kingdom of God.

Did you know, for instance, that joy is one of the rights inherent to citizens of God's kingdom? Listen to this description of the kingdom of God from Romans 14: "The kingdom of God is not a matter of eating and drinking, but of righteousness, peace and joy in the Holy Spirit" (v. 17).

That is amazing news! Think about it for a moment.

It doesn't matter how many mistakes you have made . . . or how much you have lost.

It doesn't matter how much you have (or don't have) in your bank account . . . or what others have to say about you.

As a citizen of the kingdom of heaven, nothing—*nothing*—can take away your right to joy.

So open your heart wide today, friend. Don't wait until you think you deserve it, or until your circumstances take a turn for the better.

Receive Christ's joy. It is rightfully yours!

> *Remember your true citizenship: you are a child of the King of kings, and knowing His joy is your right.*

~⧉ Five Minutes in the Word ⧉~

You are no longer foreigners and strangers, but fellow citizens with God's people and also members of his household, built on the foundation of the apostles and prophets, with Christ Jesus himself as the chief cornerstone.

Ephesians 2:19–20

If we live, we live for the Lord; and if we die, we die for the Lord. So, whether we live or die, we belong to the Lord.

Romans 14:8

Praise be to the God and Father of our Lord Jesus Christ! In his great mercy he has given us new birth into a living hope through the resurrection of Jesus Christ from the dead, and into an inheritance that can never perish, spoil or fade. This inheritance is kept in heaven for you, who through faith are shielded by God's power until the coming of the salvation that is ready to be revealed in the last time.

1 Peter 1:3–5

The LORD takes delight in his people; he crowns the humble with victory. Let his faithful people rejoice in this honor and sing for joy on their beds.

Psalm 149:4–5

God told them, "I've never quit loving you and never will. Expect love, love, and more love!"

Jeremiah 31:3 THE MESSAGE

The Best Medicine

*W**hat is this?* I wondered. *Am I witnessing mass hysteria? Did I forget to take my medication?*

The roomful of people walked about bowing to one another. None of them spoke but all of them were laughing uncontrollably. A full minute ticked by on the clock, then five . . . then ten . . . And the laughter rolled on.

Maybe everyone had lost their minds.

Or maybe not.

Everyone in the euphoric group was actually in the fight of their lives against cancer. As part of their treatment, they had come together for Laughter Therapy.[29]

It sounds a little bit ludicrous at first, doesn't it? After all, cancer is a formidable enemy. Wouldn't it make better sense to show up for battle with a more menacing weapon than a good belly laugh?

Some health care professionals aren't so sure. They point to the benefits of laughter: it strengthens our immune system, improves circulation, and helps us manage pain. Apparently there is truth to the old saying, "Laughter is the best medicine."

God Himself first spoke that truth long, long ago. Proverbs 17:22 says, "A cheerful heart is good medicine, but a crushed spirit dries up the bones."

The word *cheerful* here can also be translated "joyful." You may have considered some of the emotional, spiritual, and even mental benefits of living a joyful life, but did you know that the Great Healer has prescribed joy as good medicine for your body too?

Life offers many challenging and beautiful paths to joy, but don't ever forget this very simple one: a heart that is ready to embrace the gift of laughter.

Theologian Reinhold Niebuhr once wrote, "Humor is, in fact, a prelude to faith; and laughter is the beginning of prayer."[30] Now, of course, many circumstances are not laughing matters; for those, only faith is up to the task. But often, when faced with challenges and even suffering, as those folks fighting cancer knew, a good sense of humor can be key. Laughter can defuse tension in our relationships, release stress, and remind us not to take ourselves too seriously. In the process, it also opens up space for joy!

Why not give it a try today? The next time a friend or family member irritates you, or someone cuts you off in traffic, or some other frustration comes close to stealing your joy, laugh it off. Don't let it have power over you. Let yourself lighten up instead.

Think of the funniest joke you've ever heard and let the good times roll.

Imagine your cat in a tuxedo or your husband in a hula skirt!

Picture your best friend making that goofy face that always makes you giggle.

I think you'll find that the promise of Proverbs is still true. A cheerful heart *is* good medicine for your mind, your heart, and your body too!

> **Commit to having a daily dose of laughter!**

⊱ Five Minutes in the Word ⊰

He will yet fill your mouth with laughter and your lips with shouts of joy.

Job 8:21

A happy heart makes the face cheerful, but heartache crushes the spirit.

Proverbs 15:13

When the Lord restored the fortunes of Zion, we were like those
who dreamed. Our mouths were filled with laughter.

Psalm 126:1–2

Light in a messenger's eyes brings joy to the heart,
and good news gives health to the bones.

Proverbs 15:30

May the righteous be glad and rejoice before
God; may they be happy and joyful.

Psalm 68:3

Irrepressible Life

My son named him *Hamtaro*. For a hamster he had quite a skill set. We'd put him inside his acrylic ball, and off he would go, round and round the kitchen table with our two dogs in hot pursuit. Christian's favorite thing to do was to watch Hamtaro eat baby carrots. I say *eat*, but it was really more of a storage situation. That one furry, little critter could stuff at least six baby carrots in his cheeks.

Then came a sad day for all of us . . . little Hamtaro reached the last of his days. I remember Christian holding him and saying, "I hate death. I wish we could fight it!"

In that moment Christian was beginning to grapple with one of the most painful realities of this sinful world: he was confronting mortality. Everyone will feel that frustration and heartache he expressed at one time or another, and not one of us has the power to change it. But there is One who can . . . and who did!

We read in Luke 24 that the eleven disciples were

huddled together behind locked doors. They had just endured the most harrowing twenty-four hours of their lives as they witnessed their Friend, the One they believed to be the Messiah, suffer a horrific death on the cross. I truly cannot imagine their devastation, puzzlement, and pain.

Then in a flash everything changed. Jesus suddenly appeared in the room with them. He invited them to touch His body, to feel with their own hands the miracle of His resurrection! He even ate food in front of them, further demonstrating that He was very much alive.

Yes, he had died. It was real, it was excruciating, and *it was the very death of death itself*! Luke 24:41 says that the enormity of Jesus' physical presence was almost too much for the disciples to grasp. They had trouble believing what they were seeing because they were filled with "joy and amazement."

Even today, two thousand years later, the miraculous death of death itself still has the power to fill our hearts with joy and amazement. The resurrection power of Jesus swept away all the horror of Calvary. Friday night was dark, but Sunday morning dawned in brilliant light and beauty. The tomb opened, and nothing will ever be the same again.

Jesus fought death, and He won. Because of Him, life has the final word!

> *Death has lost its sting, for Jesus is alive.*
> *And our hearts keep on rejoicing!*

⟡ Five Minutes in the Word ⟡

"Don't be alarmed," [the angel] said. "You are looking for Jesus the Nazarene, who was crucified. He has risen! He is not here. See the place where they laid him."

Mark 16:6

When the kindness and love of God our Savior appeared, he saved us, not because of righteous things we had done, but because of his mercy. He saved us through the washing of rebirth and renewal by the Holy Spirit, whom he poured out on us generously through Jesus Christ our Savior, so that, having been justified by his grace, we might become heirs having the hope of eternal life.

Titus 3:4–7

You died, and your life is now hidden with Christ in God. When Christ, who is your life, appears, then you also will appear with him in glory.

Colossians 3:3–4

Keep yourselves in God's love as you wait for the mercy of our Lord Jesus Christ to bring you to eternal life.

Jude v. 21

A Wondrous Creation

From somewhere in the darkness, the endless *nothingness*, a song began.

In one of his novels, *The Magician's Nephew*, C. S. Lewis depicts God calling His creation into life in this way . . . not through action or spoken word, but through song. The darkness of the new world lifts as He sings the stars into being one by one. After a moment, His song changes a bit and trees sprout up from the earth. Then the notes dip and soar again, prompting waves of grass to ripple along the dry ground.

A character from another world witnesses this creation moment. His awestruck response is, "Glory be! I'd ha' been a better man all my life if I'd known there were things like this."[31]

The magnificence of the natural world holds the power to bring joy to the heart of even the person who gives no thought to God at all, but how much more joy it brings to those of us who follow Christ as our Savior. The creation, like a mirror, reflects the beauty of its great Creator.

The structure and fragrance of a rose . . .

The delicate design of a snowflake . . .

The amazing inner workings of the human body . . .

The vast varieties of creatures that fill the sky, land, and sea . . .

The majestic mountain peaks stretching into the sky . . .

The planets in their steady orbits around the sun . . .

The drama of a lightning storm . . .

When Christian was a little boy, sometimes I'd take a blanket outside at night, and we would lie side by side, gazing at the expanse of countless stars above. I would remind him that God placed each star in the sky and called them all by name.

"He is the awesomest!" he'd whisper.

All around us creation shouts out the glorious news that the God we serve is a God of outrageous creativity.

And so we lift our hearts in praise to our Creator.

Standing in awe of His creativity and beauty . . .

Resting in His power and goodness . . .

Rejoicing in our majestic God.

> *Let God's glory take your breath away!*

﹏᧞᎓ Five Minutes in the Word ᎓᧞﹏

"Behold, I am doing a new thing; now it springs forth, do you not perceive
it? I will make a way in the wilderness and rivers in the desert. The wild
beasts will honor me, the jackals and the ostriches, for I give water in
the wilderness, rivers in the desert, to give drink to my chosen people, the
people whom I formed for myself that they might declare my praise."

Isaiah 43:19–21 ESV

When I look at your heavens, the work of your fingers, the moon
and the stars, which you have set in place, what is man that you
are mindful of him, and the son of man that you care for him?

Psalm 8:3–4 ESV

You, O LORD, have made me glad by your work; at the
works of your hands I sing for joy. How great are your
works, O LORD! Your thoughts are very deep!

Psalm 92:4–5 ESV

In the beginning God created the heavens and the earth.

Genesis 1:1

Great is our Lord and mighty in power; his understanding has no limit.

Psalm 147:5

Radiant Joy

I have a tip for you.

Whenever you are having a really bad day, take a minute to search online for pictures of Nelson Mandela. Picture after picture shows Mr. Mandela beaming. His face radiated joy!

President of South Africa from 1994 to 1999, Nelson Mandela was awarded the Nobel Peace Prize in 1993. He received this prestigious honor for his lifelong work to bring an end to apartheid in South Africa. In one of the most remarkable chapters of his story, Mandela deliberately utilized his support of the white national rugby team to unite his nation that was so bitterly divided along racial lines.[32]

Mandela once summed up his personal philosophy about promoting peace like this: "If you want to make peace with your enemy, you have to work with your enemy. Then he becomes your partner."[33] That strategy certainly proved effective for him! It's difficult to imagine what

South Africa would be like today if he hadn't gone to such great lengths to bring healing and peace to his country.

That's why I think of his joyful smile whenever I read Proverbs 12:20, which says, "Deceit is in the hearts of those who plot evil, but those who promote peace have joy."

But I don't think promoting peace is the most natural thing for many of us to do. Anytime we are in relationship with others, we are bound to be hurt sooner or later. It's easy to become bitter and angry. If we aren't careful, we can find ourselves saying and doing things that cause further division and brokenness.

As Christ-followers, you and I are called to something different, something better. We are to exchange bitterness for forgiveness and words that hurt for words that heal.

When we choose the path of peace, we are imitating our Savior, the Prince of Peace. We get to work alongside Him to bring restoration and healing to our world. And Proverbs 12:20 promises us that this path will bring us joy.

Nelson Mandela had many legitimate reasons to be bitter. He was in prison for twenty-seven years as punishment for his pursuit of freedom for his fellow Africans. Can you imagine? Add twenty-seven years to your age now to get just a glimpse of how long that really is. Mandela could have emerged from those prison doors filled with the rage of decades, setting everything in his path on fire.

But instead, he chose peace. Mandela walked out of those prison gates with a smile and the deep joy that comes from choosing peace over revenge.

> *Those who seek peace are truly blessed . . .*
> *and truly God's children.*

⁓❦ Five Minutes in the Word ❦⁓

There is one whose rash words are like sword thrusts,
but the tongue of the wise brings healing.
Proverbs 12:18 ESV

Gracious words are a honeycomb, sweet to
the soul and healing to the bones.
Proverbs 16:24

Turn from evil and do good; seek peace and pursue it.

Psalm 34:14

*When the L*ORD *takes pleasure in anyone's way, he causes their enemies to make peace with them.*

Proverbs 16:7

Consider the blameless, observe the upright; a future awaits those who seek peace.

Psalm 37:37

Even When Nothing
Goes Right

*H*ow hard could painting be? I thought.

I went to our local art supply store and bought a canvas, a few brushes, and some acrylic paint. Then I set myself up in a sunny spot in our den and stared at the blank canvas for a while, wondering what I should grace it with. I eventually went with a scene of a horse standing at the edge of the ocean. *Go big or go home*, I reasoned.

I worked all day and was just finishing up the sunset reflections on the water when my husband came home. I asked Barry to close his eyes as I escorted him into the den for the big reveal.

"I've taken up painting," I announced. "Open your eyes and tell me what you see."

He was quiet for a moment, then said, "It's lovely . . . but why did you paint a saddle on a lizard?" We laughed for a long time. Yep, my Van Gogh days tanked when they'd hardly begun.

But some "big fails" in life aren't so funny. Investing time and effort in causes that matter deeply to us—whether in work, relationships, or ministry—only to see them falter can be disheartening, even devastating.

Paul and Barnabas knew what it was like to face this kind of big fail in ministry. Things were looking pretty promising in Acts 13 as they worked hard to spread the good news of Jesus' love. We read, "The word of the Lord spread through the whole region" (v. 49), ample evidence that their hard work was bearing fruit. Then verse 50 begins with the heart-stopping word *But*.

It's just a tiny word, only three letters, but for Paul and Barnabas, it was the beginning of their big fail. With breathtaking swiftness, the successful work they had been doing for the Lord came to an end. One minute everything was going great. The next, violent persecution rose up and they were thrown out of the city.

Just like that, their thriving ministry was over.

If you were in Paul's and Barnabas's sandals, how would you have felt? Disappointed? Angry? Depressed? All those emotions would be perfectly reasonable! But that isn't what happened. Verse 52 tells us "the disciples were filled with joy and with the Holy Spirit."

Wow!

And *what*? How?

The presence of the great Comforter, the Holy Spirit, in their lives is the only explanation. No matter what troubles came along, the Source of inexhaustible joy was always available to Paul and Barnabas. And the two men relied on Him.

I want to be like Paul and Barnabas when I face failure. Instead of sinking into the mire of disappointment, I want to tap into the Spirit's power and exchange weakness for strength, fear for courage, and weeping for rejoicing.

I am so thankful for the Holy Spirit. He brings joy into our lives . . . even on the days when nothing goes right.

> *Celebrate the joy God promises, for we*
> *are loved whether we succeed or fail.*

❧ Five Minutes in the Word ❧

This was [John the Baptist's] message: "After me comes the one more powerful
than I, the straps of whose sandals I am not worthy to stoop down and untie.
I baptize you with water, but he will baptize you with the Holy Spirit."
Mark 1:7–8

"All this I have spoken while still with you. But the Advocate, the
Holy Spirit, whom the Father will send in my name, will teach you
all things and will remind you of everything I have said to you."
John 14:25–26

Jesus said, "Peace be with you! As the Father has sent me, I am sending you."
And with that he breathed on them and said, "Receive the Holy Spirit."
John 20:21–22

By this we know that we abide in him and he in
us, because he has given us of his Spirit.
1 John 4:13 ESV

Take the helmet of salvation and the sword of
the Spirit, which is the word of God.
Ephesians 6:17

Notes

1. Henri Nouwen, "Daily Meditation: Choosing Blessings," Henri Nouwen Society, September 8, 2015, http://wp.henrinouwen.org /daily_meditation_blog/?p=4015.
2. "I Just Hugged the Man Who Murdered My Son," *StoryCorps*, accessed February 17, 2016, http://storycorps.org/listen/mary -johnson-and-oshea-israel/.
3. Nick Vujicic, "No Arms, No Legs, No Worries," *YouTube*, February 28, 2012, https://www.youtube.com/watch?v=8jhcxOhI MAQ#action=share.
4. Rowan Williams, *Being Christian: Baptism, Bible, Eucharist, Prayer* (Grand Rapids, MI: Eerdmans, 2014), 48.
5. Thomas Merton, *Contemplative Prayer* (New York: Doubleday Religion, 1969), xiii.
6. Ron Moseley, *Yeshua: A Guide to the Real Jesus and the Original Church* (Clarksville, MD: Messianic Jewish Publisher, 1996), 35.
7. "Brian Welch," *I Am Second*, accessed February 17, 2016, http://www .iamsecond.com/seconds/brian-welch/.
8. Matt Sloane, Jason Hanna, and Dana Ford, "'Never, Ever Give Up': Diana Nyad Completes Historic Cuba-to-Florida Swim," *CNN.com*, September 3, 2013, http://www.cnn.com/2013/09/02/world/americas /diana-nyad-cuba-florida-swim/index.html.
9. "Introduction to Philemon," *Archeological Study Bible* (Grand Rapids, MI: The Zondervan Corporation, 2005), 1977.

10. Bill Adler, comp., *Ask Billy Graham: The World's Best-Loved Preacher Answers Your Most Important Questions* (Nashville, TN: Thomas Nelson, 2007), 216.

11. William Barclay, *The Gospel of John* (Norwich, Scotland: Saint Andrew Press, 1964), 181.

12. Osmund Thorpe, trans., *The Biography of Saint Gemma Galgani* (London: Catholic Way Publishing, 2013).

13. Ibid.

14. John Burnett, "When the Sky Ran Dry," *Texas Monthly*, July 2012, http://www.texasmonthly.com/articles/when-the-sky-ran-dry/#st hash.OHgARCq1.dpuf.

15. "Pietà," *Michelangelo Gallery*, accessed February 17, 2016, http://www .michelangelo-gallery.com/pieta.aspx.

16. Mike Cronin, "Pelham High School senior with special needs scores big Friday," *WMUR.com*, updated March 1, 2015, http://www .wmur.com/news/pelham-special-needs-senior-scores-big-friday /31550968.

17. George Burnham, "Billy Graham's Germany Crusade," *Chattanooga News Free Press*, July 7, 1955, https://news.google.com /newspapers?nid=860&dat=19550707&id=IXgKAAAAIBAJ&sjid =hUsDAAAAIBAJ&pg=6347,320005&hl=en.

18. "About Team Hoyt," accessed February 17, 2016, http://www.teamhoyt .com/About-Team-Hoyt.html.

19. "A Father's Love: The World's Strongest Dad," *YouTube*, December 3, 2011, https://youtu.be/ax4VIVs-qsE.

20. "Nurse Finds Her Long-Lost Father in Patient," YouTube, updated September 7, 2010, https://www.youtube.com/watch?v=x5cLaSx ZMDU.

21. Bo Stern, "Fall into Peace," *The Difference of Day* (blog), September 9, 2015, http://www.bostern.com/blog/2015/09/09/fall-into-peace/.

22. "Boy Trips in Museum and Punches Hole in Million Dollar Painting," *YouTube*, August 25, 2015, https://www.youtube.com/watch?v=Nqv2zgSM7eY.

23. *Humility*. By permission. From *Merriam-Webster's Collegiate® Dictionary, 11th Edition* © 2016 by Merriam-Webster, Inc. (www.Merriam-Webster.com).

24. *Pretension*. By permission. From *Merriam-Webster's Collegiate® Dictionary, 11th Edition* © 2016 by Merriam-Webster, Inc. (www.Merriam-Webster.com).

25. C. S. Lewis, *The Lion, the Witch and the Wardrobe* (New York: HarperCollins Publishers, 1978), 120–22.

26. N. T. Wright, *Simply Jesus: A New Vision of Who He Was, What He Did, and Why He Matters* (San Francisco: HarperOne, 2011).

27. "Rabindranath Tagore," *BrainyQuote.com*, Xplore Inc., 2015, accessed February 17, 2016, http://www.brainyquote.com/quotes/quotes/r/rabindrana 134933.html.

28. Jill Cowan, "Franklin's Dancing Cop Busts Speeders—and a Move," *Tennessean*, August 31, 2015, http://www.tennessean.com/story/news/local /williamson/franklin/2015/08/31/franklins-dancing-cop-busts-speeders -and-move/32484295/.

29. "Laughter Yoga Therapy for Cancer Patients," *YouTube*, June 14, 2013, https://www .youtube.com/watch?v=FeTVjPK4yIY.

30. Reinhold Niebuhr, *The Essential Reinhold Niebuhr* (Binghamton, NY: Yale University, 1986), 49.

31. C. S. Lewis, *The Magician's Nephew* (New York: HarperCollins Publishers, 1983), 107.

32. Associated Press, "Nelson Mandela Used Sports to Unite Racially Divided South Africa," December 5, 2013, *New York Daily News*, http://www.nydaily news.com/sports/more-sports/mandela-sports-unite-racially-divided -south-africa-article-1.1539151.

33. CNN, "Mandela in His Own Words," June 26, 2008, *CNN.com*, http://edition .cnn.com/2008/WORLD/africa/06/24/mandela.quotes/.

Want to take 5 more?

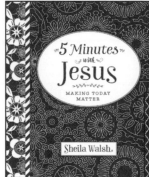

Available now

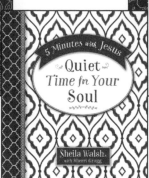

Available March 2017

Available now

Visit 5MinutesWithJesus.com to view
exclusive content and share inspiration!

Connect:

 Facebook.com/5MinWithJesus

 @5MinWithJesus

 @5MinWithJesus